WHAT CONFIDENT WOMEN DO

DAILY CHALLENGES TO SET BOUNDARIES, ESTABLISH
SELF-WORTH AND CRUSH SELF-DOUBT

KATE RICHARDSON

CONTENTS

Introduction   ix

1. WHAT'S STOPPING YOU?   1
   What's Holding You Back?   2
   Are You Confident Enough?   3
   Why Do You Struggle with Self-Confidence?   4
   Key Takeaway   4

2. ANXIETY AND YOUR BRAIN   5
   The Problem with Anxiety   5
   Types of Anxiety   6
   Can You Escape Stress?   8
   Some Techniques to Deal with Stress   8
   Key Takeaway   10

3. THOUGHT POWER   11
   Thought Patterns: What We Learn and How to   12
   Unlearn It
   How to Re-Channel Your Thought Power   13
   Key Takeaway   15

4. CHANGE THE SITUATION   17
   Search for the Positive   18
   Is It Really Impossible?   18
   Broaden Your Horizons   19
   Never Go Back   19
   Key Takeaway   20

5. WHAT SIGNALS ARE YOU GIVING OFF?   21
   What Are Vibrations?   21
   What Is the Law of Attraction?   22
   Changing Your Vibration   22
   Key Takeaway   25

6. LET GO — 27
The Empty Space Invites Goodness — 28
The Process of Letting Go — 29
Key Takeaway — 30

7. WHAT'S THE PROBLEM? — 31
Learn to Identify the Problem — 31
Employ a Problem-Solving Strategy — 32
Key Takeaway — 34

8. WHAT DO YOU REALLY WANT? — 35
Benefits of Setting Goals — 35
How to Set Attainable Goals — 36
Key Takeaway — 37

9. MENTAL REHEARSAL — 39
Visualize — 40
Create Your Own Space — 40
Visualize Your Day — 41
Visualize for Calmness — 41
Create a Vision Board — 42
Key Takeaway — 43

10. GET IT OUT OF YOUR HEAD — 45
The Art of Journaling — 46
Benefits of Journaling — 46
How to Begin Journaling — 47
Key Takeaway — 48

11. I AM AWESOME — 51
Learn to Set Boundaries — 53
Take Time Out for Self-care — 53
Set Goals and Forgive Yourself — 54
Loving and Accepting Your Body — 54
Key Takeaway — 55

12. WHAT YOUR BODY IS SAYING ABOUT YOU — 57
Building Rapport and Connection — 57
Perception — 59
Key Takeaway — 60

13. STOP PEOPLE PLEASING   61
   The Downside of People Pleasing   61
   How to Say No   62
   Key Takeaway   63

14. NO MORE COMPARING   65
   Social Media   65
   Growth   67
   Key Takeaway   68

15. YOUR INNER CIRCLE   69
   Get Rid of the Negativity   70
   Seek Out People Whose Qualities You Admire   71
   Your Social Groups   71
   Key Takeaway   71

16. BE CURIOUS   73
   Emotions and Behavior   74
   If You Allow Them to Mistreat You   74
   Key Takeaway   75

17. DRESS YOUR BEST   77
   Know Your Colors   78
   Body Shape   78
   Focus On Your Strengths   78
   Explore Your Style   78
   The Occasion   79
   Key Takeaway   79

18. PLAY THE PART   81
   What Is a Confidence Mentor?   81
   Why Does This Work?   82
   What Should You Focus on the Most?   82
   Power Posing   84
   Key Takeaway   85

19. WHY FAILING IS GOOD   87
   The Upsides of Failing   87
   We Were Born to Make Mistakes   89
   If You Don't Make Mistakes, You Don't Grow 89
   Key Takeaway   90

20. AVOID BURNOUT 91
How to Avoid Burnout 93
Key Takeaway 95

21. WHAT YOU PUT IN YOUR BODY 97
Microbiome 98
The Benefits of a Healthy Diet for Your Emotional 100
Health
Key Takeaway 100

22. MOVEMENT 101
Exercise and the Lymphatic System 102
The Importance of Daily Exercise 102
Walking in Nature 103
How Being Barefoot on the Grass Grounds You 104
Key Takeaway 105

23. MINDFULNESS 107
Cultivating Mindfulness 108
Morning Routine 109
Key Takeaway 110

24. MEDITATION 111
Rewiring the Brain 112
Implementing a Practice 113
Key Takeaway 114

25. WHAT THE HELL DO I HAVE TO BE THANKFUL FOR 115
– QUITE A LOT ACTUALLY
Find Gratitude in Your Daily Life 115
Find Gratitude in Your Shortcomings and Challenges 116
Give Back to Others 116
Key Takeaway 117

26. POWER PHRASES 119
Daily Affirmations 120
The Three Main Ideas That Hold up the Self- 121
Affirmation Theory
Daily Affirmations Benefits 121
Creating Positive Affirmations 122
Key Takeaway 122

27. DAILY WORK   125
    Meditation   125
    Yoga   126
    Journaling   127
    Listening to Music   127
    Reading   128
    Key Takeaway   128

    CONCLUSION   129

    References   131
    About the Author   143

INTRODUCTION

This book is for any woman who hasn't yet realized her self-worth. It's for the woman who feels stuck, either physically or mentally, anywhere in life. This book is for the woman who wants to feel empowered. I know what it's like to feel inadequate and undeserving. Growing up in a volatile home I tried to make myself as invisible as possible. Intentionally making myself insignificant, staying out of sight and keeping myself quiet was the only way I knew how to deal with my sometimes terrifying environment. I spent a large part of my life feeling like I didn't matter. I struggled with confidence and self-worth. I did everything I could to avoid conflict and became too much of a people pleaser. As I got older, I wanted to understand why my parents behaved that way. This sparked my interest in psychology. As I've learned more about behavior, I understand that they didn't know any better. As humans we are all doing the best we can with the tools that we have. When I look back to my parents' childhoods and see their influences and environment I understand why they were like they were. What I learned was that I didn't have to stay a product of my childhood. I could make changes to become the person I wanted to be.

Self-improvement and learning about the human mind became my passion. I have studied this for nearly 20 years. I am a qualified life coach, NLP therapist and Rapid Transformational Therapist and have qualifications in child psychology and counseling.

I decided to write this book to help other women who have lost their self-confidence regain it by guiding them through the things that have worked for me. I will show you how to find out what holds you back and how you can break free from it. I want to help you understand how to accept yourself just the way you are, because you deserve nothing less. I want you to become motivated and achieve all your goals and dreams. Most of all I want you to be strong enough to regain control of your life, decide where you want to be in the future and get there.

After you finish reading this book, my hope is that you will wake up each morning excited to discover what life has to offer you. That you will feel a sense of passion for life and eventually fall in love with yourself for who you are, the obstacles you have overcome and your never-ending potential. I am writing this book for the woman who simply struggles to cope. This is for the woman who perhaps currently doesn't like herself too much or struggles with her self-worth.

Regardless of your struggles, I promise to help you find your voice. I promise to help you know your worth and start living life on your terms.

WHAT'S STOPPING YOU?

*a*t some point in our lives most of us will experience feeling lost, stuck, even overwhelmed. There comes a time when we know what we *should* do and maybe *how* we should do it, yet we still can't seem to get anything done. There is nothing more frustrating than this feeling. To achieve our aspirations and goals, we need to rewire our thoughts and adopt better behaviors. Sometimes, all we need is to take a leap of faith, though it can be much easier said than done, especially when we don't feel ready yet.

The truth is that you will never feel ready unless you work toward fostering the habits and mindset you need to succeed. You will never take up the reins of your life unless you start to become conscious of your unhealthy behavior and thought patterns. In order to recognize and eliminate all the distractions that hold you back, learn to begin accepting yourself and understand your full potential. Realize that you are capable of achieving so many things in life, and the only thing that's stopping you is yourself, by thought processes you may not even be aware of, yet.

This chapter explores the different things that may be holding you back. It ventures into how you're the one who could be subconsciously halting your progress. After reading this chapter, you will grasp a better understanding of how confidence plays a key role in self-development and why it is that you may be lacking it.

WHAT'S HOLDING YOU BACK?

The things that hold us back are usually products of our thoughts and emotions. They may be irrational fears, unrealistic mindsets, the wrong approach, or a combination of the three. It generally takes much time and effort to discern the factors that affect your ability to move forward. However, once you do, you will be able to change the way that you interpret things. The following are the most common things that may be stopping you from achieving your goals.

Perfectionism

If you are a perfectionist, you find it hard to get on with anything in life. Perfectionism, when excessive, can quickly turn into an obsession. Being too consumed with the idea that things must turn out in a particular way or that you must be a certain way can be very tiring. Although it may seem that being a perfectionist drives you to do things correctly, it can actually make it very hard to get things done at all. Perfectionists want everything to be perfect, which is usually impossible, making it hard to enjoy and celebrate their accomplishments.

Fear of Failure

The fear of failure is success's worst enemy. You must realize that every experience comes with its risk of failure. Failure is inevitable. It is how we learn and is part of life, just like success. If you're afraid to lose, it means that you probably won't even try. It's by failing that we learn what to do differently next time to get a better result. There is a famous quote by the inventor of the lightbulb, Thomas Edison who took thousands of attempts to make the lightbulb work. He viewed it this way, "I have not **failed**. I've just found 10,000 ways that won't work." "Many of life's **failures** are people who did not realize how close they were to success when they gave up."

As a result of not trying, you will never know what you are capable of. By fearing failure, you only deny yourself the opportunity of achieving incredible things. Never underestimate yourself.

Result-Oriented

Many of us get disinterested when we don't see immediate results. This is totally normal. Humans are naturally impatient. We don't care about the journey as much as we care about the results. However, those who succeed are the ones who understand that life doesn't work that way. Seeds don't grow into fruitful plants overnight, but with nurturing and watering they soon grow into beautiful blooms. Don't get discouraged if your efforts aren't paying off right away. Remind yourself that good things are coming, and if you're doing something each day to work towards your desired outcome then it will pay off.

ARE YOU CONFIDENT ENOUGH?

Self-confidence is crucial to self-development and growth. If you are not confident enough, you may struggle to walk down the most promising paths in life. A lack of self-confidence will constantly make you question your abilities and always keep you assuming that you are not good enough. So, what is it really like to lack self-confidence?

If you struggle with your self-esteem, you may be overly sensitive to critical comments. Your insecurities may trick you into believing that others emphasize your flaws and confirm that you are incapable of doing things correctly. Insecure people also tend to adopt aggressive defense mechanisms. They may attack others for fear of being criticized. Those who have low self-esteem are more likely to develop depression, anxiety or indulge in unhealthy addictions. If you have low self-confidence, you may have trouble empathizing with other people due to being too consumed with your own problems.

WHY DO YOU STRUGGLE WITH SELF-CONFIDENCE?

When it comes to self-confidence and your inner battles, there are no rules that apply to everyone. We all respond to situations differently. What might affect someone else may not affect you. Similarly, what hurts you may not hurt someone else. However, in most cases, low self-esteem results from a childhood where significant figures in your life were overly critical. It may also result from poor academic performance, bullying and experiencing repetitive stressful events such as financial troubles or failed relationships. Those who have been subject to poor or abusive treatment from parents or partners are also likely to struggle with their self-esteem. The presence of mental and physical illnesses may also play a large role in hurting your confidence.

KEY TAKEAWAY

If you realize that you have low self-esteem, or that you have been consciously or unconsciously holding yourself back, do not be discouraged. We are human, and we can easily slip into making excuses. It's easier to tell ourselves that we don't have enough time or resources than it is to accept that the problem comes from within. However, as you read this book and begin to understand the true root of the problem, you may begin the work required to fix it. Although it may feel impossible at first, if you want to change your life, the tools in this book will guide you every step of the way.

ANXIETY AND YOUR BRAIN

$\mathcal{T}$he saying "you are what you think," is often shrugged off as another overused phrase propagated by self-help books promising to turn your life around one chapter at a time. However, this is a scientifically proven claim you'll get to learn about in this chapter. Now that you've delved deep into your psyche to understand what is holding you back, this chapter will take the analysis one step further. You'll get to see that your brain and body work hand-in-hand to trigger certain feelings and emotions based on your reactions to external stimuli. Even though this chapter will be a little heavy on science, there's no need to go digging up your high-school physics book just yet. Let's just take it one step at a time, and you'll see how it all adds up in the end.

THE PROBLEM WITH ANXIETY

Anxiety is not a condition in itself, rather it is your body's defense mechanism against stress. Anxiety is how your body copes with situations that your brain would deem uncomfortable or unsettling. People who suffer from anxiety usually experience some common symptoms that include sweating, fast heartbeat and shortness of breath. The intensity of anxiety varies greatly from one person to another. If you have anxiety, you will notice that it is activated differently according to the situation you're in and your overall emotional and mental well-being at the time. You may be wondering, if anxiety is this natural coping mechanism, then why have we been programmed to keep it at bay and fight it off at all costs? Well, the answer is simple: it's all about the context.

In healthy doses, anxiety is essential for this exhilarating pumped-up feeling that makes you want to break into a dance in the middle of the street upon hearing some good news. This kind of "positive" anxiety, as we may call it, is scientifically known as "eustress." Eustress is good for your confidence as it can do wonders in keeping your mood in check, helping you avoid negative thoughts and maintain a positive self-image.

The problem happens when the stress is negative and anxiety tends to get out of hand. Immediately, your body releases stress hormones like cortisol and adrenaline, gearing up for fight, flight or freeze mode. While this might have helped our ancestors survive the wrath of medieval beasts, today, it doesn't serve us much. With the blood retracting from the brain to reach vital body organs and limbs, preparing you to run away from danger, your decision-making centers are left compromised, and you fall into a state of fearful fogginess. You no longer have control over your thoughts, and you're more subject to displaying erratic behavior.

Remember when you had an important presentation at work, and right before you got on stage, you started sweating profusely and lost your train of thought leading you to reschedule the meeting? It had nothing to do with your professional aptitude or how unprepared you were. It was only your brain acting on a primal whim because it simply didn't know better.

TYPES OF ANXIETY

As mentioned above, anxiety comes in different shapes and forms. Many people fail to see the link between some of the most common disorders and anxiety. Meaning they can go for years before realizing that what they're suffering from is a byproduct of stress. Some of the common types of anxiety include:

Phobia

Phobia is a feeling of an intense, mostly irrational fear of some object, place, or even a situation that triggers anxious behaviors. Some phobias are familiar, like "claustrophobia," a fear of closed spaces, and "acrophobia," the fear of heights. However, there are some unconventional phobias on the far end of the spectrum, like the fear of laughter, known as "geliophobia." As you might expect, common phobias are somewhat easier to deal with and control.

Obsessive-Compulsive Disorder (OCD)

This might come as a surprise, but you can actually blame your irrational hygiene tendencies on anxiety. You resort to scrubbing your bathtub five times a day because there are some internal fears and issues you haven't dealt with or kept suppressed for so long. Consequently, over cleaning is one of the ways that these suppressions manifest.

Social Anxiety Disorder

This is a frustrating anxiety because of the social element. Dealing with anxiety is challenging enough, but when your anxiety becomes apparent in social settings with other people there to witness it, an even bigger problem arises.

In your journey to build your self-confidence, consider taking the time to identify the type(s) of anxiety that you suffer from. Even if you were never clinically diagnosed, it helps to give your anxiety a name in order to know how to deal with it and treat it in a more specific manner.

CAN YOU ESCAPE STRESS?

If stress is the nemesis, why aren't we looking for ways to escape it? To shun it out of our lives once and for all? Well, the truth is that there will always be elements of stress to deal with. However, while you can't control what is going on outside, you can very much control your thoughts to stop reacting to stress with anxiety. By learning some simple breathing and meditation techniques, you can completely change your body's old ways of reacting and train it to become more accepting of whatever environment you are in without engaging in the dreadful fight, flight or freeze response.

SOME TECHNIQUES TO DEAL WITH STRESS

Here you'll find answers to these challenges that will guide you in your quest to bring out the confident woman already on the inside. Below are some techniques to use whenever you feel stress taking over.

1. Use Your Breath

Breathing techniques have been practiced to alter the state of mind, and shift the perspective towards a more positive mindset to help cultivate better attitudes, and consequently, more self-confidence. The key is to learn how to observe your thoughts to recognize when things are getting out of control. One of the great breathing techniques is Pranayama, a yogic method that entails breathing in and out from each nostril separately. Close your right nostril with your right thumb and inhale deeply through your left nostril. Then, close your left nostril with your right ring and pinky fingers, exhale through the right nostril, and alternate. After a few rounds, you will notice that your mind has considerably slowed down, and you have better control over your thoughts.

2. Step Outside

Fresh air and the warm sunlight shining on your face is a great natural cure for stress. Especially if you work in a closed office, make it a point to take at least a 15-minute break outside every couple of hours, where possible, to recharge. This will help protect you from reacting to stressful situations in an extreme and unpredictable manner.

3. Stretch or Sweat It Out

Whichever you find more relaxing and puts your mind at ease, go for it. If you're more into the steady and slow pace, try stretching for at least 15 minutes every day to reap the benefits of your practice. However, if you prefer intense workouts to sweat your stress away, then high-intensity training or an outdoor run can be the answer to your mental woes. Whatever you choose, aim for consistency if you want to maintain long-term results.

4. Ask for Help

As a woman, this must be one of the hardest things that we must do. Like many, you believe that you're supposed to be on top of everything going on at home, like juggling work with school drop-offs and pickups, cooking and cleaning and keeping on top of birthdays and social events. Somehow you were made to believe that a good wife or mother is expected to handle it all without even flinching. However, this kind of thinking alone is outdated, unhelpful and can cause major anxiety attacks leaving you feeling unsure of your worth. If you want to become less stressed, first recognize when you are starting to feel stressed and make it a habit to ask for help whenever you need it. Whether you're at work or at home, there's no point in spreading yourself too thinly to the point of depletion.

KEY TAKEAWAY

Your thoughts directly impact how you carry yourself and affect how you interact with the world and other people.

Your body's responses to the chemical reactions happening on the inside are not the end of the story. With some practice, you can become aware of your unhelpful thinking and instead change your thoughts to support you, therefore changing your brain's old ways to more helpful neural patterns.

Stress cannot be eliminated from your life. Instead, learn some techniques that can help you deal with it efficiently.

THOUGHT POWER

*M*any women have struggled to keep a positive attitude when dealing with life's responsibilities for as long as they can remember. Whether you're struggling with society's expectations, self-esteem, self-loathe, or any other issue you can think of, these issues act like chains attached to our souls. When another obstacle appears out of nowhere, it's yet another load upon our shoulders. Negative emotions that were already brewing inside will eventually intensify to a point where they will be impossible to ignore. The delicate balance you could have achieved breaks down, and you're left wondering how you allowed yourself to get this far. Over and over again, the scenario always seems to have the same result. Even when you try to fix your routine like exercising more often or eating healthier, you still end up returning to your old ways.

Trying to change your negative behavior at a surface level won't get you as far as you would like in your self-discovery journey. Tackling the issue from the root source may seem difficult at first glance, and it's normal to feel overwhelmed about taking action. However, once you understand how your brain has a fundamental role in the way you act and interact with yourself and others, you will focus your efforts on crucial areas to improve your empowerment process.

THOUGHT PATTERNS: WHAT WE LEARN AND HOW TO UNLEARN IT

Most women may not realize how much their thoughts heavily impact their emotions and feelings. Even if their thoughts are running idle in their brains while they deal with their daily responsibilities, the thoughts significantly impact their behavior.

We humans aren't as logical as we would like to think. After all, we are social mammals that thrive in groups, and we all grow up with certain rules and beliefs that we learn from our social circles, whether it's with our families, at school, or with our group of friends. We watch and imitate our peers, trying to understand how social norms work, and through interactions with other people, girls from a very young age internalize how to behave in certain settings in order to "fit in". As a result of this continuous process, our brain creates neural connections unconsciously, and that's how we form our thought patterns that shape the way we feel which affects how we behave.

Becoming aware of how your brain has created these thought patterns is the first step towards changing them. You need to realize what type of thoughts are pushing you through your daily tasks. From the moment you wake up these thoughts start to shape your feelings and emotions, and subsequently drive your behavior in a specific direction. They're also the key to understanding why certain emotions and attitudes tend to appear throughout your life, which you may not be aware of until you put a spotlight on your thought patterns.

Let's place ourselves in the following scenario. You may have learned from your family that it's super important to worry about your body. Your mother, aunts, grandparents and even your friends were always talking about choosing the best clothing to fit your body, always looking for new diets to try and "lose some extra pounds". What may have stuck with you most were their comments about your appearance or weight. Even if you're no longer hearing these comments day and night, you're still looking at yourself in the mirror and focusing on the things you don't like about yourself, which translates to *"I'm not good enough as I am"*. How many times has this thought popped into your mind during certain situations, causing you to feel terrible about yourself? How does this thought end up modifying your behavior by avoiding wearing certain clothes, attempting less healthy ways to lose weight or even trying cosmetic surgery?

When you feel an emotion like sadness or anxiety, you already have the thought that prompted the specific reaction you're feeling. Once your brain is stuck in a negative loop, these neural connections get stronger and stronger, and they start running with no control whatsoever. Of course, it doesn't help that we are constantly bombarded with harmful messages from the media and other people about how we should think, talk and behave from the moment we wake up until the moment we go to sleep.

However, there's no need to be afraid. The good news is, just like you learned these thought patterns, you have the power to unlearn them and create new neural connections that will benefit and enrich your self-discovery. It's a matter of using the right resources to reflect upon what is prompting these thoughts and how you can actively correct them once they appear.

HOW TO RE-CHANNEL YOUR THOUGHT POWER

Take a moment to assess where the root of your problematic thoughts come from. You can try a very simple exercise. Notice how you feel right now. Are you happy, sad, scared or angry? What are you thinking right now? Can you see any connection between what you feel and what you're thinking about?

Even if it's not obvious initially, the way you talk to yourself greatly influences your emotions. Find a connection between your feelings and what went through your head in the previous exercise. That's the influence I'm referring to. Your emotions are the key to what you've been thinking – helpful or unhelpful. Your thought pattern has a big impact on how you feel and act daily. If this pattern circles around being negative, critical and doubtful your emotions will mirror this attitude. That's why being conscious about your inner dialogue is so important. Would you talk to a friend the way you talk to yourself? It helps to picture yourself when you were 3 or 4 years old, as the young, innocent child you were. Would you talk to that young child in the way you talk to yourself now? That person is still you, and you don't deserve the critical, damaging self-talk you are likely feeding yourself daily.

There are different ways to keep track of your thought pattern and correct it. Here I share some methods that I've personally used and have given me great results. However, feel free to tailor them to your liking.

Physiology: Body First, Thoughts Second

Your body and your mind are feeding each other in constant feedback. Whatever you may be thinking about, your posture, facial expression and mannerisms will match it. The principle is fairly simple to understand: if you're feeling sad and worried, get up and shake your body around. If you're pacing from one place to another, breathing fast and shallow, sit down and start doing breathing exercises. The idea here is to break the loop between your thoughts and physiology so that you can change your emotional state. This approach doesn't guarantee a quick mood change. It allows you to stop the negative loop for a moment, and by altering your physiology your brain releases different chemicals that can help change how you feel. This allows you to refocus your thoughts.

Journaling: Write Down All Your Thoughts

Another good way to keep track of your thoughts and see what your inner voice is currently focused on is to have a notebook to write these thoughts down. There are different ways to do this. You can set a specific time in your schedule to sit and write about whatever comes into your mind, some people choose to do this first thing in the morning or last thing at night. You can take the notebook with you everywhere and write whenever you're able to about situations or emotions that are bothering you. The idea is to have a physical reminder to become the observer of your thoughts and what your inner voice is saying so that you become aware of your inner world or current programming. Read more about journaling later in the book.

Self-Talk: Change Your Inner Dialogue

Everyone self-talks to some degree. You can always be aware of the way you talk to yourself, no matter where you are. When you notice yourself feeling sad, low or anxious for example, it's due to what you are thinking or focused on - whether consciously or unconsciously. Take a few minutes to analyze what is going on in your head and ask yourself simple questions to redirect your train of thought. For instance, if you're thinking, *"I'm not good enough"*, you can ask yourself, *"Is this really true?" "What's the worst thing that could happen in this situation?" "What if that actually happened?"* Now you are in the process of questioning the thought rather than accepting it as true. Often we just accept our thoughts without questioning where they came from and whether they reflect reality. These thoughts can come from childhood conditioning and no longer serve you at the point you are in your life right now.

KEY TAKEAWAY

Focus on using the right internal language: language that is supportive to your goals or the person you are becoming. Treat yourself with compassion, care and respect, even when you're not in the best mood. Changing the way you refer to yourself will slowly start changing how you feel about yourself and how you act in different situations. Rewiring your brain will take time and effort, but once you can see where your limiting thought patterns are creeping in, you can change them until they become your new way of thinking naturally, and you will be closer to reaching the full potential of empowerment.

CHANGE THE SITUATION

There are many things that we can't control in life, and unfortunately, this includes situations we often find ourselves in. We can all find ourselves in less-than-ideal circumstances. By accepting these situations and learning how to deal with them life will become less stressful. Inevitably we will live through some difficult and challenging experiences. Complaining about the situation is an easier path to take. Where possible, we even try to find someone to blame. While this may be a temporary relief, it is always very exhausting in the long run. We can't live through the majority of our lives dwelling over the tough times otherwise we are living in the past and missing out on creating a better future.

The more we resent a situation, the longer we have to experience it. It's normal that you are sad sometimes, that's okay. However, every time you express your discontent, you live through the situation over and over again. Instead of feeding into the negative thoughts and feelings and letting them take over you, work toward finding solutions and perhaps making the best out of the situation. At first, you may think that it's impossible to be positive in certain situations. As you learn to change the way you look at things, instead of trying to change the situation as a whole, your brain will be programmed to find the silver lining. There are always two sides to the same coin. Every bad thing that happens comes with at least one good thing. By looking for even the tiniest, most insignificant positive aspect of the situation this may prove to be appreciable in the long run - it's the butterfly effect. This process can be referred to as "reframing" your thoughts. Reframing, in simple terms, is like changing the frame around a painting. By tweaking the frame you can see the painting from an entirely different angle or perspective. Even though the painting itself hasn't changed, the frame through which you view the picture has, which can change the entire meaning

Similarly, the situation you're in will not change, but how you perceive it will. Instead of trying to change your reality, you can endeavor to view the situation more positively. This chapter will explore how you can reframe your thoughts to view things from different and more positive perspectives.

SEARCH FOR THE POSITIVE

This may be one of the most obvious yet challenging things that you need to do to change your outlook on life. As previously explained, everything in life comes with its good and bad aspects. If you have a tendency to focus on the negative aspects your thought process could be making the situation seem more negative than it is. Thinking about the positive aspects can make you feel slightly better. If you spend more time focused on the positive side of things, you will be developing the habit to reinforce this state of mind.

It's the same with negative situations. Thinking about the positive aspects can make you feel slightly better. If you spend more time thinking about the positive side of things, you can even develop ways to reinforce them.

IS IT REALLY IMPOSSIBLE?

It is always very easy for us to tell ourselves that our dreams are impossible to achieve. You should always ask yourself whether your dreams are improbable or truly impossible. The improbable can always become possible. Life is all about dynamic possibilities, but their likelihood of occurring depends on various factors. Without effort or anything playing out in something's favor, everything is improbable. All you need to make the unlikely more likely is just one seed of potential.

BROADEN YOUR HORIZONS

Keeping an open mind is not always easy to do, especially if you don't deal so well with change. However, as soon as you start to accept that change can be good (by focusing on the positive aspects,) it will be easier to keep an open mind. If you don't broaden your horizons and take a shot in the dark, at least every once in a while, you will never move forward. You need to meet new people and take on different experiences so you can make headway. Otherwise your life will come to a standstill.

NEVER GO BACK

The key to "changing the situation" is never to let yourself fall back into the old pattern of viewing things in a negative light. It takes a lot of effort to take on a more positive outlook on life and initially there will be some old thought patterns that try to take back control. As soon as you become aware of the old thoughts creeping back in let the thought float out of your head and take on a better thought instead. By consistently doing this you will develop new neural pathways to better thinking and the old ways will fall away. This has been described to me like a path through an overgrown field. If you keep walking over it the path becomes clear and well formed. This is identical to creating new neural pathways. In the same way when you stop using the old worn path (the old way of thinking) it becomes overgrown and disappears.

KEY TAKEAWAY

It's normal to feel sad and angry when something bad occurs. However, it's not helpful to obsess over the situation and let it consume us. When we dwell in the negativity of situations, we become more likely to develop anxiety and depression. The more we let negative thoughts and emotions consume us, the harder it is to pull ourselves out of this rabbit hole. Therefore, we must work on reprogramming our brains to view things in a different light.

WHAT SIGNALS ARE YOU GIVING OFF?

The energy around you plays a significant part in determining your self-confidence. The better the energy, or signals, that you give off, the higher your self-confidence. Your thoughts and actions send out an energetic signal to the universe and those around you.

WHAT ARE VIBRATIONS?

Think of the energetic signal you give off in terms of vibrations. According to celebrated inspirational speaker Esther Hicks, your body is made of vibrating electrical energy like everything else in the world.

Everything in the universe vibrates, and you read those vibrations with your physical senses, which helps you to perceive the world around you. Ultimately, when you get down to the most minute level, we are not made of physicality – we are made of pulsating units of energy.

The vibrations we give out change depending on what we see, experience, think and feel. These vibrations then act similar to radio frequencies that people around us pick up.

Think of it this way: if you're feeling fearful or vulnerable, your vibrations signify this to the people around you. This is an issue for several reasons. Firstly, it leaves you open to the machinations of the unethical around you, who will see this as an opportunity to take advantage of you for their own gain.

Secondly, even if the people around you are not looking to take advantage, it signifies the power dynamics. You, in your vulnerable state, have the lower hand in any interaction.

Furthermore, giving off negative vibrations acts as a block to the things we want, known as the law of attraction.

WHAT IS THE LAW OF ATTRACTION?

According to the law of attraction, things that have similar vibrational natures are attracted to one another. This holds true for non-living things, as well as people.

We can only attract what vibrates in harmony with us. Therefore, if you give out negative vibrations, you will attract people, circumstances and events with similar vibrations to you. On the other hand, if you operate on a high vibration, you attract the same.

Like your five senses, your emotions also act as vibrational interpreters, allowing you to interpret the vibration of people and things around you. If you are upset or frustrated, not only will you attract things with similar vibrations, but you will also be drawn towards people with matching energy.

In practice, this concept is simple – if you're in a bad mood, you're likely to find that your day goes badly. Conversely, if you have a positive mindset, you're far more likely to have a good day.

Everything is ruled by the law of attraction, which is why paying attention to the vibration and energy you're emanating is crucial.

CHANGING YOUR VIBRATION

No matter how positive you keep yourself, the fact is, we cannot avoid negative emotions. Keeping these emotions bottled up and suppressed, even from yourself, can result in anxiety, extreme loneliness and the development of unhealthy coping mechanisms. It becomes difficult to connect with other people, as they don't understand your real emotions. It can even have physical effects, from stomach aches and weight fluctuations to constant headaches.

If you experience an adverse event in your life, you don't have to wear a positive mask for the world. Instead, take the time to grieve, work through the pain and, most importantly, begin to heal. You can do this with a therapist or mindfulness coach. By accepting the feelings instead of avoiding them you can work through this stage in a healthy way.

Staying in a negative state for an extended period of time will affect the vibration and energy around you, which can affect your self-control, and impact your ability to connect with the positive people around you.

If you find yourself unable to let go of your negative feelings and vibration, it's important to work to change your vibration. Some methods you can use include:

Meditate

Meditation doesn't only need to be about clearing your thoughts. It can also help you feel more at ease with your life, including any challenging situations you may find yourself in.

Many people find that consistent meditation has positive effects on their mindset and the vibrations they give out. In practice, you don't have to spend long hours on it – even 15 minutes daily can help. Some people meditate by going for a walk, others find being out in nature or by water can help them feel grounded or bring about inner calm. Spending some time meditating when faced with negative situations will still have a beneficial impact. Meditation and its benefits are explained in more depth further on in the book.

Gratitude

A fast way to change your vibration is to focus on the good in your life. This may be as simple as feeling grateful that you have a comfortable bed to sleep in, or you have a day off coming up. By looking for the good, you are training your brain to do the same. It will look for more good things to bring to your awareness. This in turn raises your vibration to a higher frequency.

Develop Healthy Habits

Tending to your body's physical needs benefits its spiritual requirements. Healthy habits aren't only limited to a better diet. They can include everything from meditation and exercise to journaling, visiting a therapist or a medical professional and more.

Treating your body right not only helps improve your mood and vitality it also helps you understand your self-worth. Healthy habits are a way of cherishing your body, which boosts your self-confidence.

Stop Worrying About Others

It's a common worry we all have – what are other people thinking about me? What are they saying about me?

Comparing yourself to the people around you and dwelling and worrying about this can affect your self-esteem as well as lowering your vibration. Instead of worrying about others' thoughts and actions, concentrate on yours. Acknowledge the positives in your life, as well as the achievements you have accomplished. Focus on your success and watch as you experience more of it.

Do What Brings You Joy

If the things you do are draining you instead of bringing you happiness, you'll quickly find that your energy levels dip, you lose your enthusiasm and your outlook becomes negative. Instead, make time each day to indulge in something that brings you joy.

It may not be possible to change jobs to something you love more, but you can still spend a portion of each day with a hobby or task you love. As you grow better at it, you might even find that it changes from a pure stress-reliever to something you can spend the rest of your life doing. Most importantly, it should be something that makes you happy – and when you move through the world happy, you attract people with similar energy to you.

KEY TAKEAWAY

Our bodies are more than just the physical –they are made up of electrical energy known as vibrations. These vibrations function based on the law of attraction, and you attract people and things with similar vibrations towards you. If you give out negative vibrations, indulge in something that helps you boost them, making them more positive. Options include meditation, finding things to feel grateful for, developing healthy habits, focusing less on the opinions of others and making time to do things that bring you joy.

LET GO

*R*eleasing resistance is key to healing, growth and getting everything you desire. It is in letting go that we allow what is best for us to come in. But releasing resistance is one of the most difficult things to do. Once we do this, however, we allow all the good things to flow.

When we resist, we put blinkers on and miss the goodness that exists. We stay in a place of resentment and misery. When things occur, or situations happen that are less than ideal, many of us naturally cling to the bad moments. When we lean into releasing, we come to be truly present in the moment. It is in the present moment that we find true bliss and joy. When we are present, we find that there is no real issue in our lives. In the present moment, we find that the past does not exist, it's over, and neither does the future because it hasn't happened yet. All we have is our present moment.

We can only get into the present by letting go; letting go of our expectations, egos, wounds and pain. This may seem easier said than done. When we practice getting into the present, we find that it's easier to relax, be at peace with ourselves and truly enjoy life. Life can easily pass us by if we get too stuck in the entanglements of our minds and wounds. It's hard to see the truth when we are so fixated in the limitations of our minds and allow it to rule our lives.

To let go is a conscious choice. It is a conscious decision to release. It may feel scary and painful, or you may be at the point where you cannot take any more and letting go is the only choice. The sooner you acknowledge that, the quicker you can begin to let go. To let go means to let go of trying to control everything and instead allow life to take you where it needs you, all the time staying focused on your desired end result. Our need for control can override this, and we get stuck. When we let go, we move into our heart space. We let our higher selves take over. When we resist, we fall into the ego trap. The ego tells us that our wounds and our pain need to rule.

THE EMPTY SPACE INVITES GOODNESS

Letting go is an empty space. When you let go, you say goodbye to worry and fear. You say goodbye to insecurities and doubts. You say goodbye to something that you cannot control, and by relinquishing control, you grant the universe control to bring you what is best for you. Unfortunately, when holding on so tightly to what we think is good for us, we can easily miss gems.

It is important to honor where you are and not mentally punish yourself for not being where you want to be. Letting go is a journey. It is a process, and you may need to go through the steps several times before you get to a place where you can comfortably let the mental chatter leave and be in the present.

We cannot control what happens to us. We cannot control the external, but we can control how we react to what happens to us. In this reaction, we find our power. In this space, we find our strength, and we grant ourselves the ability to transcend our wounds. When a situation threatens to affect our inner selves, it is important to develop enough space between our thoughts and the 'self' that observes our thoughts to choose our reaction consciously. You can develop this space through regular meditation. Meditation gives you the skill and insight to understand where your thoughts end and your true self begins.

It's your reaction to the external that causes internal conflict. The more you develop space between your thoughts and reaction, the less you succumb to this chain reaction. Subsequently, the less you are a slave to your thoughts, the less you will be a slave to your emotions. Instead, you are choosing your thoughts, actions and emotions from a conscious and intentional place. These are the fruits of letting go.

THE PROCESS OF LETTING GO

By resisting letting go of what you dislike, you invite in more negativity. Yet, the instant change in energy is noticeable when you decide to let go. The first step of letting go is taking control of your mind, and you can do this through meditation, single-tasking and taking regular breaks throughout the day. The second step is ensuring you have a safe outlet to express your emotions in a healthy process and work through them. It's difficult to let go if you hold onto emotions and feelings deep down and let them fester. These emotions can still control you without you realizing it.

The third step is acceptance. Through acceptance, we begin to rely on ourselves for validation or answers. For example, if your partner leaves you seemingly out of the blue, you may be left feeling abandoned, rejected, and with a lowered self-esteem. If you take a step back and begin accepting the situation, knowing that it's okay if you never know why they did it and that you truly don't need external validation, you will begin to see the positives of the situation. If you are in the middle of a breakup, you might find that this seems impossible. That's okay. It's a process, and you need the lessons that you learn at each stage. Once you get to the acceptance stage, you begin to see that you are doing better without them. They may have been bringing you down or tampering with your dreams without you even realizing it. You begin to find your true joy and voice and see that they were only a blip in the road, a lesson to mirror back to you your unresolved wounds and, ultimately, your true worth.

The fourth step is forgiveness. This can be difficult when there are people involved in the situation who may not apologize. You must reach deep inside and find the courage to forgive yourself and others in order to let go completely. From here, you can move safely to the last stage, which is staying present. In the present, we find everything we will ever need.

KEY TAKEAWAY

Letting go is a process. It's a journey, and along the way you will develop insight and integrity and begin to see yourself as you truly are. You will develop and honor your self-esteem and self-love and realize that choosing you is always worth it. Choose the present rather than reliving and staying stuck in your past, or worrying about what hasn't happened yet. Choose life over existing.

WHAT'S THE PROBLEM?

 omen are genetically predisposed to analyze issues from every possible angle. Truth be told, this can be quite helpful occasionally, as this can help identify and resolve even hidden issues. However, this analyzing tendency can also result in getting stuck circling the problem without finding a solution. You are more likely to uncover or even create new issues this way than resolve the original one. Encountering the occasional bump on the road is inevitable in everyone's life and dealing with it can help us grow as a person. The only thing that can resolve your issues is finding a suitable solution. Of course, this is often easier said than done, especially if you aren't used to some quick problem-solving techniques. Once you learn how to quickly identify the root of the problem, finding a solution will be much easier.

LEARN TO IDENTIFY THE PROBLEM

One of the most challenging parts of finding the solution to any problem is identifying its roots. Fortunately, there is an easy way to tackle this by using your emotions. Sometimes we are so focused on employing our thinking process that we simply forget to examine our feelings about what's troubling us. When in fact our emotions and instinct can be the most valuable tool in identifying any problem. After all, they are there to warn you, and you merely need to listen to them. These warning signs could be present all the time, or they might have appeared in the past and you didn't pay them attention. In any case, you will have to look deep inside yourself and analyze all of your experiences, beginning with the most recent ones and moving back toward the past until you discover the problem. Once that's done, the solution will be much easier to find.

Let's say you are arriving home from work emotionally drained every day. As there are chores waiting for you, you don't take the time to analyze your problem. You just know it's there, and it's bothering you. Since you realize the problem comes from the workplace, begin your analysis from there. When did you start to feel the way you do about your workplace? Did something in particular happen at that time? You may find that your feelings stem from a conflict with a colleague you aren't getting along with. To find a solution you will need to uncover the reason for the animosity between you both. Think about how you felt each time before every argument. Were you feeling angry at them for any reason? Did they get a promotion and you didn't? Did they fail to complete an assignment you were relying on in order to finish yours? Even if you were on good terms before, you might feel resentment towards your colleague without realizing it.

EMPLOY A PROBLEM-SOLVING STRATEGY

Another mistake people often make is employing one solution to several different issues. Even if you successfully identified your problem, you might fail to resolve it because you're stuck on one solution. For a solution to be viable, it needs to help you reach your goal and do this in a reasonable amount of time. The perfect solution should also make you feel better, and at the same time be beneficial for those around you. It should also be easy for you to devise a plan for carrying out the desired solution. If it isn't, you might want to look for a different resolution.

Essentially, the same way you used your feelings to get down to the root of the issue, you use them to resolve the problem. Going back to the previous example, besides gauging how you feel about your workplace conflict, you can also try figuring out what will make you feel better. Would being more flexible during teamwork with colleagues get you into fewer conflicts? Do you feel dissatisfied with the position you occupy at your workplace? Would you like to take on more meaningful tasks? Would changing your position or perhaps your entire workplace make you feel more like yourself? The solution could be as easy as persuading your boss to hand you more challenging goals to meet. After all, it can be very satisfying completing tasks of increasing difficulty levels that you enjoy. Being able to do that is a great way to prove to everyone, including yourself, that you are capable of handling more.

Of course, as you know, every problem can have more than one solution, you will just need to find the right one for you. Distancing yourself from the issue might help you with that, as this can make you see things more clearly. You might even realize that you would like to be on better terms with your colleague. In this case, try to get to know them better. Understanding their perspective might shine some light on the reason for the animosity between you. Additionally, it can help lighten the mood, so you will be happier to work together as a team, and not against each other in the future.

All in all, the right solution will provide you with happiness by overcoming your obstacles. While this process is essential for our general happiness, the road to achieving it can cause a lot of grief. However, if you start treating your problems as opportunities to triumph, you might spare yourself from many headaches, and you won't spend so much time analyzing the problem.

KEY TAKEAWAY

Learning how to find solutions to your issues is one of the easiest ways to build self-confidence. Whereas the rising number of hurdles has a negative effect on your self-image, solutions have the opposite effect. Consequently, you need to find more resolutions, not problems!

There are several benefits to finding solutions to your problems. The most important one is, undoubtedly, finding happiness. Being happy will make you an emotionally stable person who, in turn, will resolve issues much faster.

WHAT DO YOU REALLY WANT?

*I*f you are one of those people who likes to go with the flow, you probably consider goal setting boring. What's more, you could think this is taking the joy out of the little surprises life can throw in your direction. However, establishing the desired outcome for your future can bring many advantages to your life. It can teach you how to focus your attention and master anything you want to achieve in life. While this doesn't mean you have to plan everything you do, it is necessary go through your life establishing some goals you would like to complete. The trick is to set long and short-term targets you know you can achieve. It will help you become successful in areas of your life that you would like to improve.

BENEFITS OF SETTING GOALS

Having a sense of purpose in life can make you a much happier, more fulfilled person. Even if you are satisfied with your life right now, setting a new goal can provide you with a change of direction and a renewed sense of purpose. Who knows, maybe your new goal will direct you to a place where you will be much happier than you are right now? Sometimes it's worth taking time for some self-reflection and examining your position in life. It's never too late to change direction, and a well-determined goal will help you with that. Plus, this reflection time could help you re-evaluate your priorities too. Once you have done that, you can determine a new target leading you towards something much more important, that you truly want to achieve in life. You will avoid wasting time on unimportant things that lead you nowhere. If you set a target goal for where you want to be in your life, you will make much better decisions that will allow you to achieve that future goal.

While going with the flow for a while is a good way to relax after a stressful event, drifting aimlessly through life doesn't let you create what you want for yourself. If you want to take charge of your future, determining some new goals is a great way to do it. This way, you could have more control over where you're going and how you get there, which could mean the difference between success and failure. Besides having a huge impact on your future, a new purpose could positively affect your present. It could boost your motivation and give you something to look forward to every day until you reach your target. If you have a long-term goal, set smaller milestones along the way. These small victories provide you with motivation and sustain your passion for the long term outcome.

Finally, although your path to fulfillment could be more challenging, life with goals can be much more enjoyable. The level of happiness you feel when you achieve a particular challenge will be exhilarating. This will also have a positive effect on your self-image and make you appreciate yourself more. Sometimes achieving even seemingly insignificant goals can make you realize you are capable of much more than you thought.

HOW TO SET ATTAINABLE GOALS

When choosing something you want to achieve, it's crucial to have realistic expectations. If you've already tried your hand at something similar and failed, that should give you an idea of what not to do next time. On the other hand, not reaching your goal could just mean you need to allocate more time each week or try a different method. Maybe you didn't have sufficient planning to make every part of your plan viable. Even if you know where you want to be in life, challenging times can make you lose hope of ever getting there. If you set a goal you can achieve in smaller sections, you are much more likely to reach your long-term goals. So if you have a fairly large target, break down all the steps you will need to get there. It doesn't matter how many small steps will be required as long as they allow you to reach your desired outcome.

Another factor that could determine your success will be timing. Set yourself a realistic time frame to achieve your overall goal and the steps needed to get you there. Regular reviews of your progress will be much more likely to keep you on the right path, so make sure you fit this into your schedule. When doing this, leave allowances for any setbacks that may happen from time to time. Have a plan for any potential mishap, so you can keep yourself focused on your final outcome and not be sidetracked by nuances. As this can save you from many headaches, it's important to have your steps figured out in advance.

Even though it's important to take actions that will bring you closer to your outcome, there may be times when something happens to prevent you from doing that. Do not beat yourself up in these situations because that could hinder your chances of getting there. Instead, re-evaluate your options and choose a path that will take you closer to what you want to achieve. When you take a successful step towards victory, make sure to reward yourself for your effort. This is an important part of the process.

KEY TAKEAWAY

Setting goals for yourself gives you purpose in life. If you find yourself at a crossroads, reexamining what you want to achieve next can determine your future path. It can also help you focus on actions that will get you there more quickly.

When determining goals, you will need to make sure that they are realistic and will lead you to the outcome you want to achieve. Whether you opt for long-term targets or just a short victory, you will get what you need from it.

MENTAL REHEARSAL

*W*hether you need to build self-confidence for an upcoming event, or step on the stage to address a massive crowd, start picturing the way you want the occasion to go for a successful outcome. Experience the event in your mind before it happens. Use your senses to see yourself behaving successfully and feel the emotions you want to feel. What are you saying, what can you hear, how is the other person responding? By engaging imagery, emotions and your senses, you start activating neural networks in the brain, which is like programming your brain for success. Repeat affirmations with emotion. During this practice, you force your brain to boost its imaginative power and perform a task without actually doing it, helping you visualize the outcome you desire and gain confidence. Mental practice is effective because it follows the concept of "practicing what you want to happen," which guarantees better results. When you keep picturing something in your mind, real or imagined, it's like you are giving your brain instructions of what you want to happen, and your brain responds. When you rehearse mentally how you want things to go, you will likely gain success, which builds your confidence and keeps you inspired.

VISUALIZE

A lack of confidence and self-esteem is a negative feeling that stems from fear; for example, the fear of not being good enough, not being liked, or losing your loved ones. This negative connotation can be overcome by acknowledging the fear. For instance, meeting new people may seem scary to someone who lacks confidence. However, once you face your fear you can start easing yourself into situations where you can chat to one person for a short amount of time. You could learn some conversation starters and prepare some scenarios to have ready to excuse yourself. This way you start becoming comfortable with what was previously uncomfortable. Each time you push yourself out of your comfort zone you are expanding the levels you are comfortable with, and eventually you lose the fear of meeting new people. Similarly, when you imagine the process and outcome, you can feel more confident going into the situation.

This is where the practice of visualization comes in. The idea is to visualize things and situations as you want them to be instead of how they currently are. See situations and things as if you have already experienced them. It is really important to feel the exact emotions of the experience that you want to feel to keep you motivated and confident. Even though this practice may still leave you a little apprehensive, you will gain enough courage, motivation and confidence to take action and ultimately enhance your self-esteem. Below are some effective visualization techniques for you to try today.

CREATE YOUR OWN SPACE

When you create space for yourself, you engage all of your senses and allow your body to feel more attuned with your mind and soul. When you feel calm and peaceful you instantly gain the confidence to achieve more. The visualization practice will work more effectively if you find a space where you feel extremely comfortable and will not be interrupted. You can create your space at home or find a place outside where you won't be disturbed. When we talk about creating your own space, it does not just imply your physical space but also your mental space. You want to be able to clear your mind of negative thoughts and feel comfortable and peaceful in your space.

Follow these steps to practice visualization effectively.

1. Lay down or sit in a comfortable position and close your eyes. Relax and focus on your breathing. Take deep breaths and observe your breathing pattern until you feel the stress leaving your body, from your head to your toes.
2. Divert all your attention to your breathing and free your mind of any irrational thoughts. Next, identify a goal or situation you want to take control of.
3. Analyze this goal or situation and contemplate the next step. What is holding you back exactly? How can you overcome it? What behavior do you need to adopt, what type of person do you need to become?
4. Visualize yourself performing the task, feel the emotions you want to associate with the situation. See everything going exactly as you want it to. Repeat to yourself, "I can do this; I am unstoppable."
5. Repeat this visualization as often as you need to.

VISUALIZE YOUR DAY

Plan your day and decide the time you will spend on specific tasks depending on your schedule and productivity levels. See yourself completing each task exactly as planned. Get into the details and focus only on the positive aspects.

VISUALIZE FOR CALMNESS

Visualize your favorite scene or place to stay calm and balanced. This visualization practice is inspired by a mindfulness technique where the person feels more self-aware and complete. For example, if you like to visit the beach, visualize yourself walking barefoot on the warm sand. Engage all your senses to visualize the beautiful sunset across the horizon and feel a gentle breeze on your face. This self-awareness technique will provide the reassurance that everything is in order, thereby making you more confident.

CREATE A VISION BOARD

Vision boards are an effective and practical way to visualize your dreams, aspirations and goals. With a vision board, you are printing your dreams every day for the universe to manifest. With this practice, you can visualize the result and gain confidence and inspiration to travel the right path for the fulfilment of your goals. Vision boards provide motivation and excitement, the exact emotions to operate at a higher vibration and attract the right opportunities, people and events to bring about the outcome you desire. Your vision board is telling you that it is time to take the first step, which is a massive confidence booster. If you think you are lacking in a particular area of your life (love, career, friendships, etc.), design your goals accordingly to get where you want to be.

To make a vision board, think about your goals and aspirations. Next, find relevant images in magazines, books, or online. For instance, if your main goal is to lose weight to feel confident, find images of you at your ideal weight, those who have successfully lost weight in a healthy way, or healthy recipes you would like to cook. Cut out the images and stick them on a card or corkboard. Place the board in a location where you can see it every day and spend a couple of minutes visualizing the goals as if they have already happened. It's essential that you see yourself having achieved the goal, and feel the emotions attached to that outcome. Whether your goals are long-term or short-term, vision boards possess the power of making it happen, which is much needed to build self-confidence and stay inspired.

KEY TAKEAWAY

Visualization works towards calming your brain's irrational fears and bringing you closer to reality. It tells your mind and soul that everything is possible and you are capable of achieving your dreams, building confidence-and keeping you inspired. The idea is to focus on what you want as if it has already happened.

GET IT OUT OF YOUR HEAD

*I*f you feel stressed and have the same worries or anxious feelings taking over all the time, getting your thoughts down on paper can alleviate stress. Similarly, if you feel stuck in an area and like you need some inspiration, the act of literally getting feelings out of your head onto paper can have amazing results on making sense of what's causing any stress and worry. Writing down questions such as "how can I feel more confident at work", focuses your mind on solutions and as you write you find more answers popping into your head. This process helps you realize what thoughts are taking over, whether they are helpful, encouraging thoughts, or if they are coming from an out-of-control inner self-critic running the show. By making it a habit to write for several minutes a day, you can see what thoughts or beliefs are holding you back. Once you are aware of them you can start to eliminate them. For instance, if your current thinking pattern is, "I'm useless with money, I'm always in debt", by writing down the question, "how can I manage my money better?" your brain automatically looks for answers. In the same way if you say to yourself, "why am I so useless?", your brain will come up with reasons why you are useless. Ask yourself helpful questions that create ideas of how to improve or change. You'll find once you start writing, the answers will come flooding to you because you are helping to direct your mind. It is also a good way to keep a track of your achievements and focus on what you are grateful for.

THE ART OF JOURNALING

The idea of journaling is simple - putting your thoughts on paper helps clear your mind from thought clutter. If you commit to jotting things down on paper, you will become aware of any limiting patterns of behavior emerging.

You can rely on journaling to improve your accountability and take on new things. Writing down things helps you get a reality check that impacts your psychological well-being and confronts your excuses, making you more honest with yourself. For some, activities like baking, singing, painting, etc., feel more therapeutic and release their emotions. Similarly, journaling lets you get things off your chest and assists you in productive thinking.

The effects of journaling are so profound that even successful businessmen and women, entrepreneurs, and gurus use it daily. It helps them stay enlightened and confident. In fact, journaling has been around for centuries. This practice provides a versatile tool that enables you to stick to a routine, organise your thoughts and boost your creativity.

BENEFITS OF JOURNALING

The three main benefits of journaling-

1. Crystallizes Your Mind Notes

Writing, in general, helps you get more attuned to your mind and thoughts. This is why students are asked to make notes when study-ing. When you sit down to journal, you are replaying your past events to extract relevance and confront reality. In this way you can learn from your mistakes and review your experiences to live a better future with confidence.

2. It Feels Like Therapy

Your journal is like your best friend. You can rant to it without being judged. Pick up your pen and jot down all your thoughts without thinking twice. Journaling is an effective way to relieve stress and alleviate anxiety. While a therapist provides a specific time for you to unload and finish talking, a journal provides optimum freedom and no time restrictions for you to unload your frustrations. Journaling is so effective that even experts rely on this practice to treat patients during Cognitive Behavioral Therapy (CBT.)

3. Decipher a Thought Pattern

At times, we cannot comprehend the peculiar nature of happenings in our daily lives. Our mind becomes numb, and we just stare at the void, sometimes completely helpless. If you have been in this situation before and have struggled with your emotions, journaling is for you. It helps you decipher a thought pattern and makes you more self-aware. This practice also helps you uncover solutions and tweak your thinking patterns to manage your life more successfully. As we keep writing, we automatically find solutions or options for our problems. In turn, it helps break the pattern and get rid of unwanted thoughts and fears.

HOW TO BEGIN JOURNALING

You can write as and when you feel like it, or you can determine the amount of time you want to dedicate and decide how often you will write. While some prefer journaling twice a day, others write only once or twice a week. The time you invest will entirely depend on you. Journaling should not take up a significant part of your day. All you need is 10 to 15 minutes (or longer if you prefer) to narrate your daily occurrences, thoughts, achievements and frustrations. When you see your frustrations written down it can take the impact out of them.

Invest in a bullet journal or use a regular notebook and use your journal as you please. You could also make a digital journal as some people find it easier to write, save and keep their notes secure. Irrespective of the medium or tools you choose, your journal can be used for various things and you may want to decide on just one of these initially, for instance whether it will be related to task observations, deciphering your thought pattern, or uncovering your daily frustrations in order to eliminate them, with the help of this book.

The key is to stick to this practice and encourage yourself to do it every day. You can also find several interesting templates online and make your journal from scratch.

Repeating a pattern, behavior, or practice for 21 days can easily turn into a habit. If you are still skeptical about the actual effects of journaling, try doing it for at least 21 days and see the results for yourself. After the first 21 days, you will automatically be tempted to continue this practice as it has become a habit. Note that creating the right environment is crucial to stick to this habit, which includes considering your mindset (your mind should be ready to journal,) taking your daily schedule into account, and decluttering your physical environment. All these aspects are necessary to be mind-ready and begin journaling.

As you record and review your thoughts, you will be prompted to prioritize your daily actions to ones that bring you joy or closer to your goals, and to focus on specific areas to build confidence. You will be able to tell the difference between important and not so essential episodes in your life.

KEY TAKEAWAY

Journaling helps get you closer to your thoughts. It can act like personal therapy, especially when you read back over your notes a few days later and you can start to see patterns of behavior or realize things that made you mad were not really that important. Since this practice relieves stress and anxiety, it makes you more confident and motivates you to keep growing.

I AM AWESOME

$\mathcal{Y}$es, this is the mantra to repeat to yourself every day, especially when you feel that you are not good enough. Instead of beating yourself up, shift your energy and focus on to the positive aspects of your life. Looking for things to be grateful for when you feel anger, fear or frustration changes your energy levels and releases different 'healthier' chemicals into your body. This may seem easier said than done, but if you truly delve deeper into your soul and your inner blueprint, you will realize that self-love and self-acceptance is important for a happier life and healthy well-being.

Self-love

Self-love and self-praise are two important terms to understand and manifest in your life. If you don't value yourself enough to love who you are, exactly how you are, how can anyone else? When you acknowledge yourself for something good that you achieve and praise yourself inwardly, or reward yourself with a treat, it reinforces self-love. Both self-love and praise lead to a healthy self-esteem and confidence. When you give off that kind of confidence other people treat you in the same way. Have you noticed when someone seems to have low confidence, others also treat them with little care or respect? This may be happening to you currently. Sometimes people with low self-esteem are even referred to as a doormat when they let people walk over them because they are unable to say no or set boundaries.

Most of the time, the way others treat you reflects what you believe deep down that you deserve. I'm not talking about people that use violence, verbal or sexual abuse, as they are generally in need of therapy to deal with what makes them behave that way. I'm talking about 'ordinary' friends, neighbors, colleagues, even strangers. These could be beliefs that you currently are not aware of. It could be sub-conscious programming based on how you were treated as a child, or other past experiences. If you don't value yourself enough, not many others will bother to recognize your skills or your worth. Each time you do a good job or achieve something, spend a moment acknowl-edging it and even congratulating yourself. However, if you fail to fulfill a task as well as you wanted to learn from it, think what you will do differently next time and move on. Strive to learn and improve instead of beating yourself up.

While the practice of loving yourself helps you feel more confi-dent, as mentioned, it also determines the type of people and relation-ships you attract. Your image at work, your personality at dates, and your behavior during social events will drastically change once you start appreciating yourself. You will walk with a sense of confidence and snatch the authority from others who put you down. More importantly, you will learn to cope with your life problems and bounce back with full energy.

I've been repeating the term "self-love" over and over again, but what does it mean exactly? When you love yourself, you don't just feel good but also valued. You are thankful for your existence, your life, your body and your relationships. Self-love stems from a series of continuous and consecutive actions you take to grow spiritually and psychologically. This dynamic state is achieved only after multiple stages of acceptance where you acknowledge your strengths and areas for growth. More importantly, you live with courage and avoid explaining your drawbacks. For those that may be suffering with low self-esteem, it can feel a big leap to go to 'loving' yourself. If, at first, you struggle with the term self-love change it to liking yourself. By appreciating yourself for the good things you do, and by starting to affirm to yourself "Each day I like myself more and more" you can start to rise from self-dislike to liking and then loving and accepting yourself.

When you practice self-love, you instantly feel compassion towards others too. You acknowledge that life can be difficult for everyone, and we all try to cope with adversities in our own way. Look at these helpful tips to begin your self-love journey.

LEARN TO SET BOUNDARIES

Learn to say "no." Whether it's for work, relationships or your social life, you must keep away from activities and meetings that are stressful and deplete your energy. While helping others is a noble cause, do not make things more difficult for yourself. Saying no does not imply that you are selfish or weak. It merely means that you respect yourself enough to protect your physical, mental and spiritual health. The inability to say no to people and situations will eventually lead to burnout and exhaustion, which means you are not taking care of yourself as you could be.

TAKE TIME OUT FOR SELF-CARE

If you learn to take care of yourself, you are being compassionate to yourself. Along with fulfilling your basic needs, incorporate certain self-care steps in your routine, such as exercising, healthy eating and getting enough sleep. Furthermore, focus on your mental and spiritual health by practicing meditation or mindfulness and performing activities you enjoy. Treat yourself to your favorite food once in a while, mark out time for you each day or week to spend a couple of hours doing something for you, a bath with candles, reading a book, learning a new skill. Set a part of your monthly budget aside and buy yourself things you like. The idea is to nourish yourself as much as possible to keep your spirits high and continue appreciating yourself.

SET GOALS AND FORGIVE YOURSELF

Set a goal or an intention that will act as your driving force to move ahead. If you design a purpose, you will accept yourself more and thrust yourself into living a meaningful life. Even if your goal or purpose is not clear at the moment, keep moving and find ways to delve deeper and realize your intention. When moving forward with a strong intention, you will undoubtedly live a meaningful life and succeed with time. At the same time, forgive yourself and learn from past mistakes instead of punishing yourself. Look at mistakes as lessons rather than considering them as failures. You have a long life to live, so why not live it lovingly?

LOVING AND ACCEPTING YOUR BODY

We often beat ourselves up if we gain or lose a few pounds. A small blemish on our face freaks us out. Any form of negative connotation with our body perceived under societal norms can make us feel ashamed and embarrassed. Your height, weight, or skin color do not define you as a person. Be proud of who you are and walk with confidence.

The very fact that your body is keeping you alive is marvelous. Your heart is beating and your lungs are working hard to supply oxygen, even while you are asleep. If a pesky pathogen enters your system, your body tries its best to fight the infection and make you healthy again. It does all this automatically, without you even having to think about it. Isn't it wonderful? When you focus on the positive aspects of you, you will feel grateful to have the body you do.

The most difficult part is the acceptance stage, which is also the beginning. Once you acknowledge and commit to your body image you have already won half the battle. Living in denial will only make it worse. Instead, acknowledge and repeat to yourself, "I realize that I have a negative relationship with my body, but I want to change it." When you repeat this to yourself, really believe those words and feel the positive emotions attached to feeling great about yourself.

This realization has spread across the globe and has given rise to the "body positivity" movement that has helped women regain confidence. The crux of this issue lies in judgment. If we stop judging ourselves and others around us, the world will become kinder and more empathetic. The change must begin within yourself. If you learn to love yourself and accept your authentic self, others will be inspired to do so, too.

KEY TAKEAWAY

Repeat to yourself, "I am awesome," and don't let anyone tell you otherwise. Your body, your mind and your soul are helping you live and experience life to its fullest. Be grateful for your existence and be good to yourself. When you love yourself and feel that you are good enough, you will instantly feel more confident.

WHAT YOUR BODY IS SAYING ABOUT YOU

We all know that the majority of communication is non-verbal. Our body language and facial expressions reveal a lot about our internal state. Understanding our body language as well as others can help us connect and empathize with others better. Being aware of our body language will help us present ourselves confidently and easily. We can choose the body language that will reflect the way we want to be perceived.

In 'The Body Keeps The Score,' Dr. Bessel Van Der Kolk writes about how traumatic experiences get stuck in the body. Unprocessed traumatic experiences can cause our bodies to contract, freeze and develop a certain way to move against our nature. This manifests in us as low self-esteem and low confidence. We find that we have these blocks within us, and we cannot locate the root of them. These blocks come from our emotional blockages.

BUILDING RAPPORT AND CONNECTION

A popular NLP technique is mirroring. Many NLP enthusiasts will use this to develop rapport, connection and enhance communication with others. With mirroring, one person will attempt to, discreetly, mirror or copy the other person's general language. The theory is that this makes the other person more comfortable, although it is happening under the conscious awareness level. The person has no idea they are being mirrored but will feel connected or comfortable with whom they are speaking to. The mirroring should only be a general sense to prevent the other person from catching on, which they could easily do if they are copied almost exactly. Instead, you might want to subtly cross your legs if they cross theirs, place your hands in a similar position to theirs or match their speed and tone of voice. You only need to pick one to two things to mirror.

Humans are intrinsically drawn to other people that are similar to themselves. They will flock together in groups with those with whom they share familiarities. This aspect of human nature can be used to your advantage. Of course, the intention is never to use it to manipulate, but rather it should be used to make yourself more confident, enhance your communication and develop deeper bonds. With the right intention, it is perfectly okay to use the psychological phenomenon to develop yourself further and to manage how you appear in the world. The way you come across and how others relate to you can go a long way to improving your chances of success. The way others perceive you will affect whether they choose to develop a relationship with you, whether it be a business, romantic or friendly relationship. These connections are vital to enhancing yourself as well as your financial, business and personal success. That's why it is so important to become comfortable in your body.

When you allow yourself to truly relax, be present and be in your body, you open yourself up to smoother communication, rapport and relationship building. When you are tense, contracted and flighty, your mind cannot relax and cannot focus its efforts on socializing. Instead, all the mind and body's energy is concentrated on the nervous system response such as flight, fight, or freeze. When we heal our emotional wounds and trauma, we release the tension in the body and allow ourselves to be present. In this fast-paced world, even without the wounds or trauma, we may find it difficult to stay connected and present. It can lead to a disconnect between the mind and body. This disconnect means that our bodies are communicating our internal conflict as opposed to a strong, confident aura.

PERCEPTION

The way you express yourself through facial expressions or body language is how the world sees you. When you stand tall, physically grounded in your body and relaxed you come across very differently to someone whose shoulders are rounded, who is stuck in their mind, and physically and mentally tense. The way others perceive and treat you will often be judged by these first impressions they have of you. There may very well be a good reason why you are tense or in a low mood manifested in the way you are carrying yourself, but others don't know that. Instead, they pick up on someone who has low self-worth or low self-esteem. That's why it is vital to stay conscious of habits or body language that make you come across as low in confidence. Your energy dictates what the universe brings in.

Do a quick exercise. Sit or stand with typically bad posture, slumped over, your shoulders drooped, eyes looking down and your neck not in alignment. Observe how you feel for a couple of minutes. Then take a deep breath, stand tall, shoulders back, look up and smile. Notice how you feel now. Probably a distinct improvement in mood and mindset.

This is the frequency other people are feeling. There is an underlying energy that is aligning or misaligning us all. When you consciously become aware of how you carry yourself, you notice a huge change in how other people see you and how you feel about yourself. The way you feel about yourself influences your mood, self-esteem and thoughts. A quick and easy boost if you feel yourself in a low mood or not feeling well is to refocus your mind on what you want and not what you don't, ground yourself by standing tall with your shoulders back. Choose to take up space in the world and notice how quickly you feel your mood improve. This hack can help you whenever you notice that the day has got to you. Perhaps a bad day, combined with negative comments, has caused your body language to mirror your internal state. Start to choose differently, and your internal state will soon catch up. There is often a cycle here of external and internal circumstances that feed each other.

KEY TAKEAWAY

Body language is our way of communicating our internal state. By learning how to heal our emotional wounds, traumas and relax into ourselves, we communicate to ourselves and others that we are whole, healthy and confident.

STOP PEOPLE PLEASING

It's perfectly understandable if you feel the need to be accepted by the people who play significant roles in your life. Saying no is especially hard when it comes to your loved ones, and as much as you want to do it, you end up caving most of the time. However, you end up suppressing your desires and creating an environment where everyone else will be happy except you. Sacrificing your happiness, in turn, leads to much anxiety that significantly decreases your chances of living a successful life personally and professionally.

THE DOWNSIDE OF PEOPLE PLEASING

Believe it or not, pleasing people all the time will not make them like you more. It usually has the opposite effect as people will start to see you as someone without a personality. If you always say things to please someone, you will be seen as untrustworthy as people will never know if you are telling the truth or using flattery. It means that instead of keeping them close, your actions may push them away. Those who stay by your side could possibly do this because of their ulterior motives. They may see you as someone who is easy to manipulate, presenting them the perfect opportunity to get what they want.

If people begin to turn away from you, you will reexamine your self-worth and reach a negative conclusion. Your confidence level will drop significantly, as you convince yourself that you deserve what happened to you. You may lose touch with people, or worse, you will try to please them even more. Besides ceasing to love yourself by not making what you want matter, it may also stop you from loving the things you used to enjoy. No matter how much you like doing something, if you do it even when you don't feel like it merely to appease someone, it will make you feel resentful towards them and yourself, along with the fact that you are telling veiled lies to everyone around you.

Unfortunately, these harmful effects of misguided interactions with people can be detrimental to your mental and physical health. First, you will lose your inner peace because you will never get what you truly want. It will lower your self-confidence and, at the same time, increase your anxiety levels. If you get rejected by the people who matter the most, whether from never saying no or because you failed to please them, depression may ensue. Aside from causing mental struggles, these events will also cause physical symptoms. You will be more prone to migraines, stomach issues and high blood pressure.

HOW TO SAY NO

If you want to learn how to stop people pleasing, you can use several different techniques. To gain more confidence practice different scenarios by sitting in front of the mirror and thinking up the best responses you can use in each scenario. The response you use will depend on the situation. For example, if your employer asks you to do something and you are already swamped, you could say, "I'm happy to do this, but I already have these projects to complete. How would you like me to prioritize this work?" This will show that you are committed to the workplace while refusing to take on everything on your own.

Let's say that a friend calls you to ask if they can come over for a catch up on your day off. Your natural reaction would be to agree because you don't like to upset your friends. However, you've had an incredibly stressful week and you really need your day off to recharge and have some time to switch off. If you don't feel like agreeing on this occasion, you don't have to. You can say something like, "I'm sorry, I can't today. I've had a difficult week and I need some time for myself." You can then offer an alternative such as, "but I'm available on Saturday and would love to meet you then if you're free?" A good friend will understand and the fact that you have offered an alternative shows them that you do want to see them, but you just cannot make it today.

When it comes to family members, especially older relatives, this may become a little trickier. Of course you don't want to disappoint them, so you try to appease them as much as possible. There are always those who know your weaknesses and aren't afraid to use them against you. If you want to say no to these family members, you can. You just need to find a polite way to do it. Say something like, "I'm sorry I don't have time to help you now, but I can quickly explain how you can resolve the problem by yourself". Or, if they ask for you to do a specific thing, you can say, "I'm not confident I can do that but I can help you find someone who can". They may feel a little put out at first, but they will learn to respect your boundaries and understand that you have a busy life and can't always do things immediately. You will be pleased because you have successfully said no, which probably took some courage, and you've avoided doing something that would have added to your already swamped day.

KEY TAKEAWAY

While it doesn't hurt to please your loved ones from time to time, constantly doing so to your own detriment isn't beneficial for your well-being. For this reason, avoid suppressing your desires and aim to live your life according to your choices.

Practice saying no in front of a mirror by thinking up several scenarios where this might be necessary. If you truly don't feel that you must do something, everyone from friends and family to your boss should get no for an answer.

NO MORE COMPARING

Comparison is the root of low self-esteem. When we compare ourselves to others, we focus a laser on the highlights of their life, which, on the one hand, is great. We should be able to celebrate others and their achievements. The harmful effects happen when we begin to compare ourselves, internally and externally, to others. Whether we know them or not, or they are a friend or a social media influencer.

SOCIAL MEDIA

In this social media age, we are exposed to so many different peoples' lives. Gaining insight into others and how they live has never been easier. Our minds are slowly conditioned to think that we know these people, although we never have and may never lay eyes on them in real life. We experience a distorted version of reality through this, one where we are the side characters in our lives. One where we think we aren't wealthy enough, pretty enough, or fashionable enough. The comparison rarely stops at these superficial levels. Even those who consider themselves above these social standards compare their spiritual journeys to others.

Once again, social media gives us a special insight into other people's lives. On the one hand, it allows us to connect more intimately with others, but, on the other hand, it gives us more material to compare ourselves to others. These comparisons can erode your self-esteem because you ultimately compare yourself to someone you don't truly know. You don't know their background, upbringing, or privileges. You don't know the blessings or hardships they have experienced. Instead, you only know what they choose to show you, and that's not to say that they are manipulative or untruthful. It is their prerogative of what they choose to share with others.

When we compare, we ignore another person's true reality and instead imprint our insecurities onto them. This projection only makes us feel worse and contributes to a cycle of low self-esteem or confidence. The inferiority you feel is a result of feeling that you just can't quite match up. This feeling essentially stems from misconception because you can never truly know what another person is feeling or their internal state. What is portrayed can never be a true reflection of themselves, and that's okay. While there is probably more scope on social media for people to be more unfiltered and vulnerable, how we feel about ourselves and how we let others affect us is our responsibility. Choosing ourselves how we feel can easily prevent other people's actions from having any effect on us. This way, we take back our power and stop giving it away to others.

It is important to realize that you are unique. As 'cliché' as it sounds, it's true. There is no other soul who is like you on this earth. You are inherently worthy. No other person can bring to the table what your essence brings. No one else can be who you are. That is your special sauce. A great exercise to embody this is to spend a few moments everyday basking in this. Wholeheartedly, take in this truth and allow it to fill every cell of your body. Know that you are one of a kind, that no one could ever be you. You are part of the cosmos. A living, breathing human who is part of this planet.

By comparing yourself to others, you disregard your inherent worth. You are too good, too pure and too true to compare yourself to anyone, no matter how incredible you think they are. Acknowledge and revere others for who they are, but at the same time, do not allow it to affect how you feel about yourself. Ultimately, it is a waste of your emotional and mental resources because of your uniqueness. There will be others who admire qualities about you that you dismiss as unimportant.

GROWTH

An alternative to a comparison habit you may have is observing the gap between yourself and where others are. You may witness the places where you can grow, or gain insight into what your soul truly desires. This is a more helpful way to think as it can help us understand that we can have the things others have if that's what we truly want. Without witnessing it in others, we may not know these are things we truly desire. That is why it is important to 'study' or associate with people who are further ahead of where you want to be as this is how you can shortcut your own journey, by learning how they have accomplished things and avoiding their pitfalls.

The more you work on your self-concept and self-esteem, the more you discern between what is a fruitless comparison or your soul telling you, "I want this". You might want to begin a simple exercise where you question these thoughts. Do you notice yourself stuck in a negative loop of comparison, or is there a soulful feeling emerging where you feel inspired or uplifted by the possibilities of having this in your life? It might even take a while to tell the difference between the two, and sometimes the difference is very subtle. The more you examine yourself and the more intimate you get with yourself, the easier it becomes to understand what is negative and what is in alignment with your purpose.

Acknowledging your inherent worthiness is important to combat comparison. Often, we rely on achievements or the external that are only reflections of societal standards to make ourselves feel better.

For example, we might call on the fact that we graduated or that we are deemed pretty, which is fine. However, when we only rely on these external factors for validation, we completely miss our true essence. Coming from a place of respect for yourself and understanding that you are worthy merely because you exist, you can then compile external achievements.

KEY TAKEAWAY

Embodying these thoughts and ideas, you will realize that it's much easier to drop negative thought patterns, such as comparison. When you have a true self-love and esteem foundation, other people cannot bring out insecurity or negativity within you. It will no longer bother you as you become stronger mentally and emotionally.

You will even find that you have a greater capacity for joy, love and ease as you understand just how worthy you are.

YOUR INNER CIRCLE

*I*t shouldn't come as a surprise that the people you surround yourself with have a huge impact on your life. People with whom you spend most of your time, make up the type of person you will become. Having good friends in your life makes things easier. Good social relations with other people tend to bring out the best in us. Wisely choosing your company and letting go of those who do not enhance your life is not always easy. The first step is recognizing the difference is to consider who uplifts you and who has the type of energy that brings you down? There are many people you can hang out with, and they'll be there for you. Many people want to have as many friends as humanly possible, not knowing that quality far outweighs quantity when it comes to friends. Out of all your friends, the most important group is your inner circle.

Your inner circle molds your life. You share the important things with them and ask them for advice. They seem like the kind of people who will always be there for you no matter what. They tend to stick with you through thick and thin and always have your back. Having too many friends could mean that you end up having many acquaintances but very few genuine friendships. You may be familiar with the concept that there is a difference between knowing people and being friends with them. Having a small circle means that you'll spend more time with each person individually, and you develop higher levels of trust. Your genuine friends may not always agree with you, which is good because the relationship is strong enough to be compassionately honest, whilst knowing they want the best for you.

We tend to be attracted to people who are like us, who have the same outlook and qualities, or have qualities we admire. These are the people we are likely to have as friends. Spending more time with fewer people makes you trust them more, and your loyalty towards these people increases by a great margin.

GET RID OF THE NEGATIVITY

Life isn't a bed of roses. Sometimes it's easy to do things, and other times it's not so easy. In life, it doesn't matter how hard you are hit. What matters is how quickly you can recover and keep moving forward. Progress is the name of the game. Don't just go through life, grow through it. Growth is the only guarantee that tomorrow will be better. However, to grow, you must first eliminate negativity from your life. You may have that one friend who is always being negative. The pessimistic one in the circle always has problems and tends to make other people around them negative as well. The people you surround yourself with have a huge effect on your mood and your personality. When you spend time with people, you tend to pick up habits intentionally or unintentionally. When that one friend is always negative and pessimistic, instead of cheering you up or making you happy, they make you negative as well, or lower your energy.

These people can't help themselves, and the worst part is they drag you down along with them. You want friends you have fun with and enjoy being with. Friends you can share your happiness with as well as sharing any insecurities, people you trust. Surround yourself with people who bring something good to your life, and who you do the same for.

SEEK OUT PEOPLE WHOSE QUALITIES YOU ADMIRE

There is always room for improvement in your life. Find people whose qualities you admire and like. Learn from these people. It may be a normal quality you want to adopt or a certain skill set you want to acquire. You can always learn from your friends and the right ones will always support you. Work towards becoming the person you've always wanted to be by becoming friends with someone you want to be like. Success always leaves clues. Seek like-minded people out and adopt their qualities and special skills so that you can be a better version of yourself, while being authentic.

YOUR SOCIAL GROUPS

Learning and adopting the qualities that support our growth is different to copying someone entirely. If you copy others to try and be that person, you are doing this from a state of unworthiness because you are denying the person you are. Be friends with people who like you for who you are, people you are confident with and with whom you can easily communicate. Once you're in a group that understands you, then you can prosper. Your social groups need to consist of people you're comfortable with. Once you find these people, you'll see your life turn around. Suddenly life won't be so hard because you'll have people to talk to and ask for advice whenever you need it. Handling life will be easier because you'll know in your heart that you're not alone.

KEY TAKEAWAY

In a nutshell, the people you spend most of your time with will be responsible for the type of person you become. So, make sure you choose the best people to support you.

- Avoid pessimists as much as you can. In case you do encounter them, don't let their thoughts affect your mood.

- Choose quality over quantity, there are people who claim to be your friend but would be nowhere to be found when you really needed them. Make genuine and real connections with a handful of people.
- Surround yourself with people who inspire you and adopt their best qualities so that you can be a better version of yourself.

BE CURIOUS

$\mathcal{W}$e all have our bad days. The only difference is that everyone deals with unpleasant situations differently. Some people may try to cheer themselves up, talk to a friend, or accept the situation and move on, while others may get angry or lash out. Although their behavior may be unwanted, we should accept that we all lose control of our actions from time to time due to harsh circumstances. However, this is not to say that you should always make excuses for the behavior of others. Recurrent bad actions with no valid and reasonable underlying causes or justifications are inexcusable.

Understanding why people behave the way they do is very important. It will help you determine whether they're going through a rough patch or it's simply toxic behavior. Exploring beneath the surface of others' actions will allow you to understand how or if you can help them. In some circumstances it could be that you are unintentionally allowing them to mistreat you. This chapter explores the different reasons why people behave the way they do and what you can do in return.

EMOTIONS AND BEHAVIOR

To understand why people behave a certain way, you must comprehend the relationship between their emotions and behavior. While you can speculate why someone is behaving a certain way, you can never be entirely sure of the reason behind their actions. This is why you should allow yourself to get curious and search beneath the surface of what could be causing this behavior. For instance, ask common friends if this person has been behaving that way with them too. Ask the person if anything is bothering them. If this doesn't help, retrace your interactions or reflect on their recent life events. If you're sure that there's nothing that may be negatively affecting your friend, then you need to evaluate whether you want to hang out with them, or if you are the one who is allowing them to treat you poorly.

IF YOU ALLOW THEM TO MISTREAT YOU

You may be subconsciously reinforcing people's negative behavior toward you if you deeply believe that you're the only person who can understand them. You may also be too invested in them and aware of their potential, hoping that one day they will be aware of it too. You may believe that you can change them for the better. Understand that it is not your duty to change anyone. Also, keep in mind that change comes from within. You can't change someone who doesn't want to change. Everyone is responsible for their own actions. You may only be focusing on the good in them and excusing them of all their bad actions. Another reason why you may feel comfortable around them is that they can verify how you feel about yourself. For instance, if you think you are a failure, they will make you feel and believe that you are. One of the most common and hardest reasons you allow that person to mistreat you is that you are afraid to let them go. To break this cycle, you must first identify why you let this happen and proceed to set boundaries and limits, even if this will drive you apart. With the help of this book recognize your worth and that you deserve to be treated well.

KEY TAKEAWAY

Everyone is entitled to lash out every now and then. We are all subject to situations that make us feel out of control, so we can always understand and empathize with others. Never jump to conclusions and assume that they are downright toxic, look below the surface. However, if you notice that their behavior is getting out of control, or if you believe that the person has no valid reasons to project this unwanted behavior toward you, then you should start reassessing your actions.

DRESS YOUR BEST

Our clothes allow us to control how other people perceive us. We can choose which message we want to give off through the way we dress. For instance, many women show up to meetings in power suits and stilettos to establish confidence, power and authority. The way you dress not only affects your confidence and influence on other people, but it can also affect your actual performance. When you feel intelligent and confident, you will do things with more poise and self-reliance. When you think you look confident it will give you an esteem boost in everything you do.

Following the "fake it 'till you make it" approach, most things in life can be achieved. If you fake your confidence enough, you will eventually feel like you can take on the entire world. A great way to fake your confidence is to start with your appearance. Gaining confidence can be much easier than you think it is. However, you need to start by trusting yourself. One easy way to progress your self-esteem boost journey is treating yourself as you would treat other people, meaning that you should eliminate all negative self-talk. Compliment yourself and notice all the things that you like about yourself. At first, it will feel like complete nonsense, but dressing for the part and in clothes that make you feel and look different can be a great help. This chapter will explore how you can boost your confidence levels through your outfits.

KNOW YOUR COLORS

Your first step toward dressing with more confidence is knowing the colors that look best on you. Our skin differs in color, tone and undertones. Therefore, some colors look stunning on some skin tones, while others can end up washing the person out. Always keep in mind that it's okay if certain colors don't necessarily flatter your complexion. Wearing the colors that you love and complement your skin tone will make you feel confident.

BODY SHAPE

When dressing your best, know your body shape and learn how to complement it. We are all differently proportioned and sized. Dressing in a way that's flattering to your body shape will help you feel awesome.

FOCUS ON YOUR STRENGTHS

Style is subjective but looking great and well put together is not. No matter your style, playing out your strengths in color and silhouette will leave you with a clean, sleek outfit. Find out which types of clothing, patterns, prints and garment fits will emphasize your best features. Consider the various aspects of your body and experiment with clothing that makes the most out of them.

EXPLORE YOUR STYLE

Changing it up a little and challenging yourself with bolder choices every once in a while is a good idea. Try experimenting with different styles that will work in your favor for confidence and comfort. In some cases, you may find that your comfort and style extend way beyond the borders you have restricted yourself to.

THE OCCASION

To dress your best, dress according to the occasion. If you go somewhere looking either overdressed or underdressed, it can significantly hinder your confidence. Make sure to understand the type of place or event you are going to, so you may dress accordingly.

KEY TAKEAWAY

Knowing that you look your best will automatically affect the way that you feel about yourself. When you look confident, you feel confident and you end up radiating confidence. It will also influence the way that other people see you.

PLAY THE PART

*O*nce again, when it comes to the phrase, "fake it 'till you make it," it turns out that it holds true when talking about ways to boost your self-confidence and other areas of your life.

Most people hear the phrase and take it to mean pretending to be self-confident when they're not. However, that raises a question – if you aren't self-confident, how can you pretend to be? What actions can you take to fool the people around you and those you interact with – and even, perhaps, yourself?

The answer is simple – seek out a confidence mentor.

WHAT IS A CONFIDENCE MENTOR?

A confidence mentor, or a confidence role model, is someone you can look up to and emulate. This person doesn't have to be someone you know in real life – it can be a famous person whose confidence you admire, like Serena Williams or Michelle Obama.

It should ideally be someone whose behavior you can study and mirror. Take notes on how they deal with challenging situations and how they carry themselves. You can also consider how they communicate with the people around them and respond to situations when they are wrong.

If you do choose to emulate a person you know, you don't have to tell them that you're using them as inspiration if you would rather not. However, it can be beneficial to ask them for help if possible. Not only can it help you bond with them, it can also help you understand how they think, which helps your mirroring.

WHY DOES THIS WORK?

Mirroring another person's confidence helps you build your self-confidence due to something known as self-perception theory.

We normally think that our actions are affected by the type of people we innately are. So if someone is a compassionate person, they will behave compassionately towards others. However, self-perception theory holds that the reverse is true as well.

It means that we observe how we behave and then decide on the type of people we are. For example, if you read a book daily, you may decide that you're a book lover. If you return a lost wallet full of money you found on the street, you'll decide that you're honest and trustworthy.

So, by pretending to be self-confident and emulating the actions of confident people, we trick our brains into thinking that we are self-confident. This breaks the pattern of our habitual 'unconfident' behavior, and as we act differently to our normal behavior patterns we start building new neural pathways, encouraging our brain to think and act differently. It's what the concept of "fake it 'till you make it" is built on – that, at some point, the act will stop being an act and will instead become the truth.

WHAT SHOULD YOU FOCUS ON THE MOST?

So, you've chosen a confidence mentor to emulate. However, humans are complex beings. How do you decide what facets of their personality you should focus on mirroring most?

If you're asking yourself this question, consider paying attention to the following traits.

Verbal Cues

How does your role model talk to the people around them?

Even if you don't meet another person face-to-face, the way you talk with them can tell them a lot about you. For example, speaking too fast is often seen as a sign of nervousness or fear, while speaking too slow may indicate that you aren't well-versed in the topic.

Instead, pay attention to the way your chosen mentor communicates verbally. What tone does their voice take? How fast do they speak? Do they change the way they speak depending on who they are speaking to? All of these will help you alter your speaking patterns, especially in interpersonal situations that require a lot of self-confidence, such as work meetings.

Physical Cues

In a face-to-face interaction, it only takes a few seconds for someone to pick up how confident, or not, the other person is feeling. For example, a nervous or doubtful person may hunch their shoulders and appear smaller than they are, while someone confident will likely have a more open posture.

As with verbal cues, pay attention to how your confidence role model acts when interacting with other people. Are they smiling and making eye contact? How do they stand – do they shift from foot to foot, or do they stand still? How do they interact with the rest of their environment and not only the person they're talking with?

The trick is to act confident while still acting naturally. Eye contact can be good, but too much starts to feel invasive and uncomfortable. You shouldn't fidget but standing too still feels like you're playing a part. Understanding how your chosen role model remains naturally confident will help you learn and reflect those actions in your life.

POWER POSING

Another way to act confident is to try something known as power posing. It's striking a posture that you associate with being powerful to boost your self-confidence.

Amy Cuddy, a social psychologist working at Harvard Business School, was one of the first proponents of this theory which was popularized by a TED Talk given by her in 2012. According to Cuddy, power posing doesn't only have a psychological impact on you. It has a physical impact as well.

She found the people who adopted high power poses were more likely to take risks and showed an increase in testosterone, a hormone associated with confidence, and a decrease in cortisol, a stress hormone. On the other hand, people who adopted low power poses showed the opposite results.

The power pose you adopt is completely dependent on what you feel is most powerful. If you're not sure what to try, here are a few popular options. You can use some of these in private to build yourself up ahead of an event or interaction.

- The "Wonder Woman" pose – named for the well-known superhero. It involves standing with your hands on your hips and your chest puffed out.
- The "Victory" pose – have you ever seen old photos of politicians celebrating an election win? They have their arms raised over their heads in a shape that resembles the letter V. The next time you achieve something noteworthy, try this pose.
- The "Loomer" pose – is a great option to try when interacting with another person. When you stand, lean forward slightly. This pose indicates that you're fully involved in the conversation and hold a dominant position.

KEY TAKEAWAY

If you're unsure how to build internal self-confidence, try emulating another person whose confidence you admire, whether it be a person you know in real life or a celebrity. Pay attention to their physical and verbal cues and try to replicate them to trick your mind into believing that you are self-confident. You can also try adopting a powerful pose to boost your self-confidence, an action known as power posing.

WHY FAILING IS GOOD

In your attempt to become more confident in your skin, you have to be willing to take some risks and try new things. Getting out of your comfort zone and opening yourself up to new things in life, although crucial for your journey, can feel quite daunting. Fear of failure is a very real thing, especially for women, who usually have to work harder than their male counterparts to prove themselves and get to where they want in life. In this chapter, you will be asked to let go of any preconceived notions you once had about the downsides of failure and how you should avoid it at all costs. Along the same lines of adopting a more positive outlook on everything, this chapter will continue opening your eyes to the benefits of failing and how those mishaps can be a blessing in disguise. All you have to do is keep an open mind and see things from a different perspective. Let's get started:

THE UPSIDES OF FAILING

Like many people, you've probably gone through life trying your best to become one of the "winners." Your parents would urge you to be the best student, best daughter and then you grew up with this distorted notion of setting your aspirations aside to become the best wife and best mother. This pristine way of living has ingrained an irrational fear of failure in our minds where we miss out on one of the most important learning techniques in life. Besides showing you the right way after having stumbled a few times, failing has several advantages that include:

- **Building Resilience**

Resilience is an essential trait that can help you navigate the inevitable challenges that life throws at you every day. Only when you befriend failure and warm up to the fact that you won't always win on the first attempt, will you build thicker skin to play the cards you're dealt no matter how bad things may initially appear. By treating failure as a learning opportunity your mind will be reprogrammed to act differently after you experience a new failure. You will pick yourself up, dust yourself off and be ready to go again with a 'tweaked' approach. It Gives You a Chance to Reinvent Yourself

If you feel like you've hit rock bottom and you've got nothing more to lose, by looking at this as an opportunity to learn the lessons you've been shown, no matter how hard, you will be more open to the idea of reinventing yourself and trying something completely out of character. Take being laid off from your job, for example. With no employment prospects on the horizon and not having another source of income to pay the bills, think outside the box. There's a very good chance you would finally take the leap and open up your own bakery business that you've always dreamed about but never dared to pursue. Only when it feels like your whole world has turned upside down can you envision different paths that once felt too scary for you to consider.

- **It Teaches You a Lot about Yourself**

If you've grown up living in a bubble where your parents were constantly shielding you from the evils of inconvenience, then they've denied you the privilege of learning about failure and hardships from early on. Being used to having someone clean up your mess and not being held accountable for your mistakes is the underlying cause of your insecurities as an adult. You were never given a chance to make mistakes and learn from the consequences, so when reality hit as you grew up, you were thrown off-balance and didn't know how to be or act to get by. However, you'll be glad to know that it's not too late. There's still a chance for you to learn about the essence of the woman you are if only you make way for failure and push yourself out of your comfort zone to take the risk of doing something you've always wanted to do. With every fumble, you'll unravel something new about yourself. For instance, going through bankruptcy can open up your eyes to how you see money and what wealth essentially means to you. From there, you derive your values and code of ethics that would eventually help you live a more fulfilling life.

WE WERE BORN TO MAKE MISTAKES

Although this might seem like a bit of a stretch, failing is an indispensable aspect of life. According to ancient Chinese philosophy, the only way anything can be expressed is by having an opposite. In other words, the only way for there to be a success there has to be a failure. If you focus on this simple fact of life, you'd be more willing to embrace your failures and see them as the learning experiences they actually are. You'll stop berating yourself every time you make a "wrong" decision or go for the "wrong" choice. Allowing yourself the grace to mess up, you'd be opening a new world of possibilities where you're no longer afraid to experience life and everything that it has to offer fully.

IF YOU DON'T MAKE MISTAKES, YOU DON'T GROW

It really is that simple. If you commit to mistake-free living, know that you'll be standing in your way and stifling any growth that you would otherwise achieve. If the idea of letting loose is too scary for you, you can always take it one step at a time. Start with taking small risks that bear small chances of failure. Once you get more comfortable, start building the momentum until you are unafraid to take steps toward your passion. Work out a plan, look at various options, research the best way to do something, work out a budget if necessary, and then go for it. Believe in the best but don't be afraid to make mistakes. Review what or how it went wrong, adjust your approach and try again. Know that losing yourself is much scarier than never taking a risk in case of failure.

KEY TAKEAWAY

Don't be afraid to make mistakes and stop thinking of everything you might lose if you fail, instead think about everything you have to win, even if you lose sometimes.

Failing from time to time is the only way to ensure you are learning more about the world and about yourself to continue growing into the person you want to be.

AVOID BURNOUT

*I*n the modern era, women's lives are full of different stressors, now more than ever. Trying to prove that we can handle demanding careers while raising kids and managing our lives inside and outside the home means life can get very overwhelming. Even women who do not have kids or don't want to start a family are still pressured by society to work hard and live to certain standards or prove that they can excel in any field just like men. In the process of trying to run our lives as efficiently as possible, many women burn out and sometimes do not even know that what they are experiencing is a real thing, and it has a name.

This chapter will help you better understand the word "burnout" so you can identify it and recognize that you might be heading toward emotional and physical exhaustion. You are burned out when you feel physically and emotionally exhausted due to being stressed out for a long period. As energy gets drained from your body, you become less productive, less motivated and may feel helpless. It goes without saying that your quality of life gets affected on all levels, at home, work and your social life too. However, being burned out doesn't only affect your social life and work. It can lead to changes in your body, making you susceptible to illnesses like flu.

So how do you know that you are heading toward burnout? Well, there are some signs and indicators that might raise a flag. If you think that you are going through emotional exhaustion and it's getting to you, ask yourself these questions.

- Do I feel that every day is a bad day?
- Am I exhausted all the time?
- Do I feel that what I am doing at home or at work is a waste of energy?
- Do I feel unappreciated?
- Do I feel that what I do, no matter how hard I try, does not make any difference?
- Are my daily tasks boring or overwhelming?

Answering these questions might give you an idea that something could be wrong, and you need to stop and take a break. However, everybody goes through days where they feel drained and unwilling to get out of bed. To ensure that you are going through burnout, you need to check out these signs and symptoms.

Physical Symptoms:

- Feeling tired most of the time.
- Get sick more often.
- Muscle pain.
- Frequent headaches.
- A change in your sleep pattern.
- Change in appetite.

Emotional Symptoms:

- Self-doubt.
- Sense of failure.
- Feeling lonely and detached.
- Lack of motivation.

- A negative outlook.
- Dissatisfaction and a reduced sense of accomplishment.

Behavioral Symptoms:

- Pull out from responsibilities.
- Isolation.
- Procrastination.
- Drinking alcohol or using drugs as a way of coping.
- Trying to cope by eating.
- Taking it out on other people.
- Coming late to work and trying to leave early, or working excessively long hours to try and keep up with everything.
- Skipping work.

Since prevention is better than cure, the best thing you can do to help yourself and stay a happy, productive person is to avoid getting burned out. No matter what life throws at you or how demanding your job or home is, you must prevent yourself from getting sucked into the burnout phase.

HOW TO AVOID BURNOUT

The first thing you need to know is that delegating responsibilities is a good thing, and there is no shame in that. If you are a single parent, your children can take on responsibilities that match their age and capabilities. You might be a single woman and have to take care of everything yourself. Whether you have a partner or are single, there are some effective ways to help you avoid burnout other than delegating responsibilities.

Learn to Say "No!"

Stop and consider all of the tasks and chores that you do at work and home. Then, ask yourself, "Are they all necessary?" The answer, of course, is no. There is a lot of invisible labor that we do every day. Go through your daily tasks and eliminate the unnecessary ones as they eventually add up and become a heavy load, even though they seem like small tasks. Since we are different women leading different lives, I cannot define what is unnecessary for you, but to give you an example, coordinating carpools is unnecessary as someone else could do it. It's not the end of the world if you refuse to add it to your daily tasks. Learn how to refuse and stop doing small tasks that are not important but add to your workload.

Set Reasonable Standards

Let go of unrealistic standards. We are only human, and we need help from each other. It's fine if things are not perfect or the way you want them to be exactly. You do not have to put everything in place all the time. If you're tired, then you are tired! When your kids help out in their own way, which might not be perfect, let it go and show them appreciation. No one can do it all, so accept the help of others even if it might not be perfect help and thank them for it. Give yourself a break and let go of perfectionism because in real life, nothing is perfect, and that is perfectly fine!

Me Time

Scheduling me-time is as important as regular medical checkups. You are a priority, and you cannot become a giver unless you have the energy to give. Stressing yourself out and sacrificing all of your time and effort to your family or career is not a virtue. Eventually you will collapse mentally, emotionally and physically because things do not work that way. Take care of yourself and schedule a time to do things you enjoy, like a hobby, the gym, or just doing nothing at all, whatever works for you. Having me-time is essential for your emotional and physical well-being.

KEY TAKEAWAY

Women wear many hats in their lives, and if it makes you happy, that's great. However, you need to learn when to take a break. Being the best wife, mom, or employee doesn't mean that you must sacrifice your life. Taking care of your mental, emotional and physical health should be the top of your responsibilities, and will ensure you're in peak condition to manage the things you want to.

WHAT YOU PUT IN YOUR BODY

*H*ave you ever wondered why we say, "I feel butterflies in my stomach?" or "I had a gut-wrenching experience?" Well, because it is kind of true. Our brain is connected to our gut. Therefore, when we are anxious or scared, our brain sends signals to our gut and, in turn, it reacts to these emotions. Moreover, it goes both ways because the stomach sends signals to the brain, too. That is why people with intestinal distress can become anxious or stressed. In other words, stress and anxiety can occur as a result of intestinal distress or its product.

Many people go to their physicians because they experience gastrointestinal distress. However, there is nothing physically wrong with them. In cases like these, doctors rule out illnesses and refer the patients to psychologists. Psychosocial factors influence the physiology of the gut. Therefore, what you put in your body surely will affect the way you feel and your emotional well-being.

MICROBIOME

What Is the Microbiome, and Why Is It Important?

Let me tell you about a genetic material essential for our immunity, development and nutrition. The microbiome is a new discovery since it wasn't discovered until 1990. You will be amazed when you know how important it is and how it affects our bodies.

We are mostly microbes. There are more than one hundred trillion microbes in and on our bodies. That is even more than our body cells. Most of these microbes live in the gut, to be more specific, in the large intestine. The genetic material of all the viruses, fungi, protozoa, bacteria and microbes that live inside and on our bodies is the microbiome. It helps digest food, protects against disease-causing bacteria, produces vitamins and regulates the immune system. The microbiome consists of potentially harmful and helpful microbes, and if your body is healthy, they peacefully coexist together without causing any illnesses. It is important to note that if diets, prolonged use of antibiotics, or infection disrupt this balance our bodies will become prone to diseases.

The first time we were exposed to microbes was when we passed through our mothers' birth canal. Some might suggest that the womb was the first place. Either way, as we grew, our gut microbes produced more microbial species. Whether the change in the microbiome is good or bad for us depends on what we eat and environmental exposures.

The microbiome affects our bodies in different ways like:

- Digesting fibers while producing fatty acids that maintain a healthy gut.
- Digesting healthy sugars while breastfeeding helps us grow.
- Gut microbiome might affect our nervous system, as suggested by new research controlling brain functions.

- Controlling the way our immune systems work and how we respond to infections.
- Chemicals produced by some bacteria found in the gut microbiome can result in blockage of the arteries.
- The microbiome has a role in controlling blood sugar.

Foods Good for Your Gut Health

You can improve your gut microbiome by eating various foods, especially fruits and legumes, for better health. Eating fermented foods containing healthy bacteria, prebiotic-rich foods that help grow healthy bacteria, and whole grains will help improve your gut health. As for newborns, they should be breastfed for at least six months to develop a gut microbiome.

So, what types of food are good for your gut health? Many foods taste good and are also good for your insides like,

- Almonds: They are rich in fiber and fatty acids. Due to their probiotic properties, your gut bacteria will love them.
- Yogurt: It is full of friendly bacteria (probiotics). However, it is best to eat yogurt with low sugar content. Yogurt drinks have more bacteria in them than regular yogurt.
- Olive Oil: It can reduce gut inflammation and contains fatty acids and polyphenols that make it perfect for maintaining a healthy gut.
- Bananas: They are full of fiber and healthy minerals. Bananas are considered one of the healthiest snacks.
- Ginger: Ginger stimulates digestion and aids in producing stomach acids. The best way to consume ginger is by grating fresh ginger in drinks (hot and cold), soups, and any food you like.
- Garlic: It has so many health benefits to the gut as it has antibacterial and antifungal properties that balance yeast in the gut. Consuming garlic keeps harmful bacteria under control and improves gut function.

- Brussel Sprouts: They contain sulfur compounds that fight unhealthy bacteria, and fibers good for helpful bacteria in the gut.
- Peas: They are rich in soluble and insoluble fibers, which help maintain balance in the gut system.

THE BENEFITS OF A HEALTHY DIET FOR YOUR EMOTIONAL HEALTH

Now you know that there is a strong connection between your brain and your gut, called the "second brain." Therefore, it makes sense that if you are feeling down most of the time or sluggish but not suffering from an illness, you are probably not eating healthy food. Healthy food helps grow healthy bacteria in the gut, which has a positive effect on the production of the neurotransmitter. On the other hand, consuming sugars and junk food feeds the bad bacteria in the gut, resulting in inflammation and hindering the production of neuro-transmitters. Studies suggest that a healthy diet can help alleviate depression and anxiety symptoms.

Start by making a few changes in your diet, and little by little you will be able to switch to a healthy diet. Remember, any small change will have a positive effect on your health. Staying hydrated does wonders to your mental and physical health, too, so don't forget to drink plenty of water every day. Sticking to a healthy diet, drinking enough water and not skipping meals will help you experience fewer emotional fluctuations and boost your mood.

KEY TAKEAWAY

Keep in mind that we are what we eat. What you put in your body will definitely affect your physical state and your emotional state. To become a happier person you need to be mindful of what you eat and listen to your gut.

MOVEMENT

Other than eating healthy food, exercising will help you feel better by boosting your mood. Exercise helps treat mild and moderate depression and anxiety and is related to better moods for many reasons including, increasing serotonin and endorphins levels, limits the impact of stress on your mental health and helps you sleep better, which in turn, protects your brain from damage.

Here are some of the positive effects of exercise on your state of mind:

- Improves your self-esteem.
- Boosts your immune system.
- Increases your energy levels.
- Serve as a distraction from ruminating thoughts that increase anxiety and depression.
- You feel happier after working out.
- You see changes in your body shape which makes you feel good.
- Gives you a sense of accomplishment.

EXERCISE AND THE LYMPHATIC SYSTEM

The lymphatic system is part of your circulatory system. It is a waste removal service. One of its functions, and the most important one, is transporting white blood cells (lymphocytes) in the lymphatic system to combat infections and illnesses. If it is weak, it will make you more prone to diseases.

A jammed lymphatic system can result in a combination of symptoms like dry skin, cold feet and hands, aggravated allergies, bloating, water retention and brain fog. However, exercising and regular workouts will treat your jammed lymphatic system. To put it simply, being active is the cure.

To move fluids in lymph vessels, we need to move about. The lymphatic system is different from the arterial system, which automatically transports the fluids via a built-in pump. This is how amazing our bodies are and how important it is to be active. A sedentary lifestyle and lack of movement causes lymphostatic edema, which is a blockage that leads to swelling in the neck due to the accumulation of toxins.

A bad mood, anxiety and depression can result from the inability of your brain to get rid of toxins efficiently. When you cannot manage or handle strong emotions like worry and grief, a toxic buildup can manifest in the form of joint pain, getting sick more often, or gaining weight. Therefore, your emotions are connected to your lymphatic system too. In other words, to increase your lymph flow, you need to do any form of exercise during the day like walking, dancing, even jumping, so do whatever works for you.

THE IMPORTANCE OF DAILY EXERCISE

Daily exercising is not limited to weight loss, as there are many reasons why we need to move and work out every day. However, these exercises do not have to be vigorous. Daily walks or practicing yoga can be all that your body needs to heal physically and emotionally. Here are some of the reasons why you need to exercise daily:

1. To become a happier person because exercising releases endorphins, providing you with a natural high.
2. To reduce PMS symptoms. Although you might feel that this is not the time of the month to perform any physical exercise. Exercising will help you by alleviating the cramps, pain and grumpiness.
3. To improve your cognitive functions and strengthen your memory. It can be as simple as taking daily walks to improve your brain function and memory.
4. To break the fatigue cycle you need to get moving, and once you start, you will become more energetic to fight exhaustion and lack of motivation.
5. Exercising helps you sleep better at night, which is crucial for maintaining a healthy body and mind.
6. Regular exercise even gives your creativity a boost, so whenever you get stuck during a project try taking a walk or going for a bike ride to get inspired.
7. To reduce the risk of heart disease. About eight million women die from heart disease each year worldwide. However, regular exercise will strengthen your heart and reduce your stress levels, reducing your chances of a heart attack.
8. Regular exercise can make you look younger. This reason is enough to put your walking shoes on and get moving.
9. For stronger bones and muscles.
10. Boosts your self-esteem because when you look better you feel better about yourself.

WALKING IN NATURE

An easy and beneficial thing you can do for yourself is to take regular walks in nature. Whether at work or home, having a busy schedule and being stuck between doing different tasks while taking care of your family can become extremely overwhelming. A short walk in nature will help heal your body and mind.

If all you can spare is ten minutes of your time, even just a ten-minute daily walk in nature will still help you feel better. Some of the benefits of walking in nature are.

1. Fresh air revitalizes you and oxygen is vital for our brains to develop, grow and keep functioning, especially if you spend most of the day shut in your office or at home.
2. Daily walks in nature and looking at beautiful scenery are proven to enhance brain functions and increase concentration and focus.
3. Your body will get Vitamin D from the sunlight, which is extremely important for your brain, immune system and well-being.
4. To reduce stress.

HOW BEING BAREFOOT ON THE GRASS GROUNDS YOU

If you want to take your daily walks to a whole new level, walk barefoot. It might sound odd but being barefoot on the grass has many benefits. It is a therapeutic technique that helps you electrically reconnect to the earth. The earth's electrical charges positively impact our bodies, which is what grounding is all about. However, grounding is an under-researched topic, and further studies are required.

Walking barefoot is the easiest grounding technique. All you need to do is take off your shoes and walk on the grass, sand, or mud. When your skin comes into direct contact with the natural ground, you receive grounding energy. Grounding can:

- Decrease fatigue and exhaustion levels.
- Alleviate anxiety and improve mood.
- Provide better sleep.
- Lower chronic pain levels.
- Long-term grounding therapy can reduce blood pressure levels.

KEY TAKEAWAY

As you can see, being active and avoiding a sedentary lifestyle is essential for your emotional and mental well-being. Performing any physical activity daily, even if all you have is ten minutes, can improve your mental functions and boost your mood. Our lives become very busy, and we need to take care of our emotional well-being to lead a happy life.

MINDFULNESS

*M*indfulness is being fully present in the moment. It is to live life in a state of conscious awareness, mindful of your words, thoughts and actions. Notice how it's normal to go through the day in a frenzy, a blur and a series of automated thoughts and actions. But there is a better, more natural way to live your life. Being conscious in this moment, and truly present to what is taking place inside and outside of us. Despite it being a more natural, healthy and happy way to live, many of us struggle to do this. We may struggle because when we become present we face the realities of our emotions, thoughts and problems. It's a lot easier to become numb, shut down and focus on mindless chatter or allow our automated actions and thoughts to take over.

When we do that, we lose some of our power. We lose the ability to live life fully, and we resign ourselves to mediocrity. Mindfulness is the practice of consciously focusing your energy on the now. It is being in the present without judgment or critical thoughts. We may find that we can begin to edge towards this presence, but negative thoughts or judgments about ourselves accompany it. That's okay. Know that it's all a process, and it's not surprising that you're experiencing this. It's also not surprising to experience difficulty cultivating mindfulness in your life and coming across blocks. These blocks could be mental, emotional, or even physical. You might find that your body physically resists paying attention to the present and will automatically distract itself.

Many of our thoughts and actions occur to avoid feeling something or covering up another emotion. We are so used to these numbing activities that they have become normalized. It could be watching TV or Netflix for hours on end, scrolling on social media, not eating healthily, or not getting enough sunlight and fresh air. Our lifestyles now have made it difficult for us to be present without making that discipline and commitment. Of course, it also means we have many privileges that others around the world lack.

CULTIVATING MINDFULNESS

Cultivating mindfulness starts with making small promises or commitments to yourself. This is important because you begin to develop your self-esteem. Start to commit to spending the first few minutes of the day meditating. You can meditate using guided meditation or just spend a few minutes in silence focusing on your breathing. Guided meditation can be helpful if you are new to meditation and feel like you need some assistance to get into a meditative state. Meditating first thing is good because when you wake you are still in the sleepy state that makes clearing your mind of thoughts easier. Choose an area other than your bed to meditate in, if possible. Or choose another mindfulness activity.

Journaling is another great tool to use on your journey to cultivating mindfulness. You can journal each morning and allow yourself to journal your goals, dreams and manifestations. Journaling helps prime your brain to experience the future in the present, which bridges the gap between where you are and where you want to be. You can also find a ton of prompts online to journal through. This process can help you work through your emotional wounds. Journaling is a great way to process your emotions and feelings and bring greater awareness to your thoughts. By priming your brain to be aware of certain thoughts and feelings, you will notice that your brain is more aware of them throughout the day. When you wake up and go about your day without taking some time for yourself, your day can often become a blur. Whereas, when you take some time to pour energy and focus on yourself, your day is a lot smoother and intentional.

If neither meditating nor journaling works for you, try something like stretching, running, or breathwork. As long as it resonates with you, it will greatly impact you and your day. You will notice that it is easier to stay mindful on the days you wake up and are intentional with your time and energy.

MORNING ROUTINE

Developing morning rituals is important for mindfulness, but you can also continue these practices throughout the day. Try and implement practices like short meditations or journalings whenever you get the chance. It helps bring your energy back to yourself and re-center. Other ways to do this are to go on walks, breathwork or do grounding exercises, as explained in . When you notice that you are in your head, bring all your focus back into your body. You could imagine that roots are grounding your feet into the earth. Feel your feet touching the ground, or your legs and back resting against what-ever surface you're sitting on. This helps to bring more mindfulness into your day and prevents you from getting lost in your thoughts. When we get stuck in our thoughts, it is much harder to be present in the moment.

It is in the present moment that we find the truth and calmness. If we aren't living in the present we are either living in memories of the past, which has gone, or we are living in the future, which has not yet happened. By living in the past or future we are missing our life in the present moment. In the present moment we notice that we can think, feel and be with more clarity and focus. We are connected to our intu-ition, our souls and our higher selves because we are aware of what we are experiencing and can direct our focus to help create what we want. The more in tune we become with ourselves, the better decisions we can make from a place of integrity and ease.

KEY TAKEAWAY

Mindfulness doesn't need to be a scheduled practice in your life if you don't want it to be. Remember that different practices and methods work for different people. Your priority should be to cultivate more mindfulness, which can be done in any way you like. Maybe you find presence in mindfully being aware of your morning coffee. Feeling the warmth of the cup in your hands, the smell of the coffee as you raise it towards your mouth or the taste of the coffee as it makes its way into your body.

Each moment of life can be a meditation. Take the time to develop this.

MEDITATION

*M*editation is the practice of single-focus. It is a single point of focus that trains your brain and body to heal and gain mental and emotional balance and clarity.

Meditation is not only for monks; it's for the everyday person and has become extremely popular as we understand the many benefits. Meditation provides greater focus, reduces anxiety and increases creativity. These are only a few of the benefits, and for this reason implementing a meditative practice in your life is strongly recommended. Going about our everyday lives puts a lot of mental and physical stress on us if we don't do anything to release that pressure.

Throughout our days, we give away our energy through working, talking, socializing, etc. The more you give away of yourself without filling up your cup, the emptier you get. Meditation connects you back to your energy source. It provides peace of mind and inspiration. You can choose joy, ease and bliss by incorporating a meditation practice.

REWIRING THE BRAIN

Research has shown that the more we meditate, the looser certain neural pathways in the brain become. Neural pathways are developed when you do or think something repetitively. This hardens into a pathway, which means our brains begin to think those thoughts automatically. That's why rewiring your brain is important for self-development. Through meditation, we can loosen these pathways that are the root of our issues and wounds.

The medial prefrontal cortex in the brain processes information regarding ourselves and our experiences. The neural pathways from the fear parts of our brain to the medial prefrontal cortex are super strong and linked to our bodily sensations. When you experience something upsetting or scary, it causes a strong reaction in the medial prefrontal cortex, making you feel like you are under attack. We can weaken this neural pathway through meditation, which means that our reactions are not as dramatic. As we weaken this pathway, we strengthen the area in our brain that deals with reasoning, meaning that when something happens, that is scary or upsetting, we view it more rationally, helping us to become more balanced, focused and stable.

This rationality can help you make better decisions, which is why many wildly successful people rely on a regular meditation practice. The CEO of LinkedIn, Jeff Weiner, meditates daily and said that it helped him reflect better and strategize more effectively. He credits meditation for helping him "carve out time to think, as opposed to constantly reacting". It is this non-reactivity that is so important to strengthen. When we react to our emotions or external circumstances, we lose the ability to make rational, informed decisions. By making space between our thoughts we can think more logically without emotion taking over. Not that emotions are a bad thing, but they can sometimes misguide us and pollute our clarity of thought.

Emotions are just energy in motion. If we have emotions that are stuck, unprocessed or unhealed, we risk having these emotions take over and lose the ability to think clearly and accurately. Steve Jobs was also an advocate of regular meditation. Apple, to this day, encourages their employees to take out time in their day to meditate in the office. Meditation helps reduce stress and enhances creativity, so it is no surprise companies want their employees in their best shape.

Meditation helps increase gray matter in the brain, and greater gray matter means more positive emotions, better focus and emotional stability. As we age, our gray matter can decrease, meditation helps to reduce this and aids the age-related decline of cognitive functioning. If you want your brain to stay sharper and younger, add meditation to your daily routine.

IMPLEMENTING A PRACTICE

You may find it difficult at first to begin a practice. That's normal. You will come across many mental and emotional blocks because meditating means sitting by yourself and allowing whatever comes up to happen. This can be incredibly uncomfortable or downright painful at times. Start slow and build your way up. You can start with just a few minutes and slowly increase the time. As a beginner, guided meditations are a good place to start.

To get yourself in a meditative state and separate your mind and body from your day, start with simple breathwork. An easy exercise is breathing in for 4 seconds, hold for 4 seconds, breathe out for 6 seconds, and hold for 2 seconds. Repeat this until you feel relaxed enough to go into a meditative state. Another exercise is doing the above for a count of 4 (breathe in for 4, hold for 4, breath out for 4, hold for 4). While doing breathwork, focus your mind and energy on your breath and notice yourself relax.

There is no such thing as a bad meditation. You can adjust your practice to work for you. Even a couple of minutes every day will bring benefits. You may not feel a difference at first, but your brain is being rewired as beta waves decrease during meditation. Focusing on your breath is important to develop a deep practice. You might want to start by observing the air coming in and out of your nostrils, and then make its way down into your stomach, expanding your stomach, and then observe the air leaving your body. You can observe your breath at any point in the body. Perhaps one area will work better for you than another, or you can follow the breath the entire way. It's up to you, and the more you personalize it and determine what works for you, the easier and more regular your practice becomes.

KEY TAKEAWAY

Meditation is a practice. Keep showing up for yourself day after day and witness the benefits manifest in your life.

WHAT THE HELL DO I HAVE TO BE THANKFUL FOR – QUITE A LOT ACTUALLY

*D*eveloping a gratitude mindset will help you feel more confident and productive all day. You will feel happier and more positive about the life you have been blessed with when you learn to make gratitude a habit instead of complaining about what you don't have. You will appreciate your surroundings and your blessings much more than you used to. Even though developing a gratitude mindset takes time and effort, the process can be enlightening. You will also learn how to deal with negativity and feel more joyful. Practitioners have even witnessed a rise in their creativity levels once they developed a gratitude mindset. Furthermore, you develop the vision to perceive and attract better opportunities that lead to success.

FIND GRATITUDE IN YOUR DAILY LIFE

Your daily life is filled with abundant blessings and things for you to be grateful for. Simply being alive and breathing is the biggest blessing. You have a body that keeps you moving, a mind that can process your thoughts and emotions, and the senses that enable you to see, feel, smell and hear the beautiful things around you. Learn to appreciate any and every good thing in your life to develop a positive perspective and build confidence. If you delve deeper you will find multiple reasons to be grateful. Celebrating another birthday is something to be thankful for rather than feeling unhappy at being a year older. So many people have sadly not made it to your age. You have successfully lived another year which is a reason to be thankful.

You can also design a habit wherein you must think of 3 things you are grateful for. Practice this once when you wake up and once before going to sleep. To make this practice more powerful, write them down in your journal. The things you are grateful for need not necessarily be major achievements or bigger things in life. They can be as simple as food on your plate or the roof over your head. When you start acknowledging the little things in life, know that you have started developing a gratitude mindset.

FIND GRATITUDE IN YOUR SHORTCOMINGS AND CHALLENGES

While everyone is subject to difficult times, the time you take to recover and get back on your feet entirely depends on you. When combatting the curveballs that life throws at you, you must divert your focus towards the right aspects. If you learn to be thankful during difficult times as well, there is nothing that can stop you from achieving greater heights. You can easily dodge your hardships and turn the failures into lessons. While you are counting your blessings, count your failures too. If shortcomings easily defeat you, this practice is definitely for you. Simply put, sometimes you must endure failure multiple times before you can taste success, so be thankful for the learning opportunity and make the best of it.

GIVE BACK TO OTHERS

When you give back to others you instantly feel happier. The thought of making someone's day is extremely rewarding and blissful. Giving back doesn't merely imply giving material things to your loved ones and strangers. You can also express your gratitude and feelings towards them. Tell your loved ones how much they mean to you and how grateful you are to have them in your life.

KEY TAKEAWAY

When you are grateful for the things in your life by consciously acknowledging what you have to be thankful for, you begin to attract more things to be grateful for. You start looking at your surroundings with enhanced perception. If you manage to develop an 'attitude of gratitude' you can successfully change your life. While aiming for better things and higher milestones is encouraged, you must not lose appreciation for your current achievements or tiny blessings. Your family, house, loving relationships and daily meals are some things to feel grateful for. Practice gratitude daily and see the change for yourself.

POWER PHRASES

*R*epeating mantras, phrases, or affirmations, whatever you want to call them, instructs your self-conscious mind to deliver what you want, not what it thinks you want.

What you say, what you think and your internal language are all instructions you give to your subconscious. Remember what you focus on grows, you give it more power and so you get more of it. Make sure you are focused on what you want and not what you don't want. I have said this several times throughout this book as it's such an important thing to remember.

The law of attraction means that what you constantly focus on will be attracted to you - good or bad. Therefore, you need to train your brain to think positively to attract positive things into your daily life. Affirmations are part of creating the life you have always wanted and getting the law of attraction working for you, instead of against you. Do not underestimate the power of words, as they are constantly at work on your conscious and subconscious mind. Many celebrities and successful people use positive affirmations as part of their daily routine as they are one of the factors that lead them to success.

DAILY AFFIRMATIONS

In the previous chapter we talked about exercising your body and how it can lead to happiness, but in this chapter, we will discuss one form of mental exercise: affirmations. Affirmations are positive statements that reveal your goals in their completed conditions. For example, if your goal is becoming an employee of the month, keep repeating this statement every day, "I am so proud of myself as I am walking to my manager to receive the employee of the month award".

Repeating these affirmations five to ten minutes every day, allows you to program your unconscious mind to receive what you want in life. They keep you focused on your goals and help you figure out ways to achieve them and overcome any obstacles that come your way. As you go through your day you will notice that you use plenty of negative affirmations during the day, like "I never finish tasks on time" or "I can't stick to a healthy diet". This could be one of the reasons you are stuck in your place and can't achieve your goals. The best time to say your affirmations is early in the morning or before you sleep. As you say them, visualize them and feel the emotion as if they have already happened. Then take inspired action steps each day towards what you want.

Even if you do not believe in what you are saying at the start, repeating the affirmations can rewire your brain to believe in them. The concept of affirmations might seem a bit far-fetched or unrealistic. However, it does work. Affirmations are backed up by neuroscience and psychological theories. One of the popular and most important psychological theories about affirmations is "Self-Affirmation Theory". Many studies discuss the idea of positive affirmations and how they can help maintain a sense of self-integrity, which is related to our self-efficiency.

The development of these theories has led scientists to investigate if there are any changes in the brain when a person positively self-affirms. The investigations revealed that some neural pathways increase. In other words, the ventromedial prefrontal cortex that takes part in processing our self-related information and positive valuation becomes more active.

THE THREE MAIN IDEAS THAT HOLD UP THE SELF-AFFIRMATION THEORY

1. Self-affirmations are what helps us keep a global portrayal of ourselves, where we are flexible, honest, and can cope with different situations and circumstances. This allows us to perceive success more flexibly rather than fixing our perception on one idea about success.
2. Self-affirmation theory is not about how to become perfect or exceptional. It discusses that to keep a self-identity, you need to be fit and capable in various areas that you value.
3. Maintaining self-integrity is not about receiving praise but about believing that you are worthy of praise. For example, if you say, "I am a good parent." Your intention here is that you want to deserve praise, not receive it. Therefore, we keep self-integrity by doing actions that justify praise and acknowledgment.

DAILY AFFIRMATIONS BENEFITS

- Decrease stress.
- Help in recognizing alarming messages with less opposition.
- Reduce stress levels and ruminating thoughts.
- Have a positive effect on interventions leading people to increase physical effort.
- Build resilience against difficulties in life.

CREATING POSITIVE AFFIRMATIONS

When you use positive affirmations daily and commit to them, your negative thoughts will be replaced with positive thoughts and beliefs. Therefore, whenever you want to create a new reality, engulf your subconscious with pictures and thoughts of it.

So, how do you create positive affirmations? The guidelines below will help you create effective daily positive affirmations.

1. Always start by saying, "I am."
2. The affirmations should be in the present tense, not the future tense.
3. Use the positive form, and do not state what you do not want.
4. Be concise and specific.
5. Add an action verb that ends with -ing.
6. Add a dynamic emotion word.
7. Speak for yourself, not for other people.

To help you start using affirmations here are some suggestions.

1. I am brave and resilient and I can face all of life's challenges.
2. I am worthy and deserve the best in life.
3. I accept, love and value myself exactly the way I am.
4. I am awesome.
5. Every day I am getting better and better at loving myself.
6. I am doing my best, and that is amazing.

KEY TAKEAWAY

Exercising your brain is as important as exercising your body. Both lead to a healthy mental, physical and emotional state that is much needed in the fast-paced digital age we live in. You deserve to be appreciated and praised. However, you need to learn that it all starts with you and how you see yourself. Using daily affirmations won't take much of your time but can improve your life and help you become more resilient to change and difficulties in life.

DAILY WORK

*I*t is very important to keep up a high vibrational, uplifted, motivated self. Motivating yourself is a valuable skill to learn to achieve the things you want and ultimately love your life. Motivation comes in different shapes, as there are internal and external motivations. For example, you can get motivated by money or love. It's what inspires a person to achieve goals and lead a fulfilling life. To take control over the different aspects of your life you need to understand and develop your self-motivation.

If you wonder how you can keep yourself uplifted and ready for whatever life brings your way there are many techniques to choose from to help you live your life to the fullest; starting every day with intention and purpose in your heart. Below are some suggested techniques, so you might choose one or a couple adapting them to suit you and start your journey toward a better life.

MEDITATION

As previously discussed in this book, meditation works wonders for our mental, physical, and emotional states. Be sure to meditate – even for just 5 minutes. Practicing meditation every day has huge benefits.

You can start with 5 minutes and work your way up to 15 minutes, or more if you want. There are many useful meditation apps you can use to guide you through the process. I suggest morning meditations as they can make incredible changes in the way your brain and body work and set you up for the day.

YOGA

Any physical activity is extremely beneficial and will help you improve your quality of life. However, we have already discussed taking daily walks and working out, so let's talk about yoga and its benefits.

The same as meditation, yoga is an ancient practice that is backed up by science. It brings your body and mind together, creating a state of calmness and serenity. A great recipe for a healthy emotional state is practicing yoga and meditation. Find the time to practice yoga, even just a few times a week. However, if you can commit to daily practice, that would be even better. Fifteen-minute yoga practice goes a long way in improving your overall well-being. There are numerous benefits:

- Yoga is famous for promoting relaxation and alleviating stress and anxiety. It decreases the production of cortisol, which is the main stress hormone.
- Some studies have shown that yoga can reduce inflammation in the body so it can fend off pro-inflammatory diseases.
- If combined with a healthy lifestyle, yoga can decrease the risk of heart disease.
- Yoga can improve your quality of life and is used as a supplementary therapy to help people lead happier lives.
- It is recommended for those with chronic pain.
- Helps in fighting depression.
- Promotes sleep quality.
- Improves breathing.

- Increases strength, flexibility, endurance and balance.

JOURNALING

There is more to journaling other than recording and documenting memories or an outlet for self-expression. Writing can improve your health in so many ways:

- Writing a journal entry every day for fifteen to twenty minutes can reduce stress and lower your blood pressure. If you have had a stressful experience, write it down on paper. This way, you will manage it in a healthy manner by processing your feelings.
- Expressive writing can give your immune system a boost.
- Journaling promotes working memory capacity.
- Regularly writing journal entries is essential for your emotional well-being as it can improve your mood and emotional state by allowing you to make sense of what you are feeling and recognize any limiting patterns of behavior.
- Your emotional functions will become stronger and more reliable as you become in tune and connected with your needs and inner desires.

LISTENING TO MUSIC

Music feeds the heart and soul. Imagine a life without music. What a horrible place it would become. We know that music can improve our physical, mental and emotional health. Moreover, it stimulates the brain leading to better learning and many other health benefits that include:

- Improved memory.
- Helps treat mental illnesses.
- Boosts your mood.
- Brings people together.

- Reduces anxiety, depression and stress.
- Reduces fatigue.
- Enhances physical performance while exercising.
- Alleviates pain.

READING

It goes without saying that reading a good book can take you places and detach you from everything going on in your life for a while. It allows you to imagine and visualize exciting events and different worlds, boosting your mood and stimulating your brain.

Spend some time reading or listening to anything that will keep you uplifted, empowered, and feeling good. Find a hobby, practice yoga, run, hit the gym, or do anything you enjoy for at least twenty minutes each day. No matter how hard life gets, you can always lift yourself up by doing something you enjoy. These simple techniques can help you. Incorporating any of them into your life will work wonders for you and help you lead the life you deserve and desire.

KEY TAKEAWAY

Everything starts with you, even the way other people see and relate to you. You get to decide that. To lead a happy and healthy life, you need to take care of your physical, mental and emotional health.

CONCLUSION

*M*y hope is that you now see the power is within you to change your situation and create a life of purpose and fulfilment. How you view things and absorb them each day significantly impacts your life. Learning to look at things from a different, more helpful perspective and knowing your worth is key to making your life so much better, easier and exciting.

We think 60-70,000 thoughts in a day. Out of those, 90% are the same as the day before. The same thoughts lead to the same choices and behaviors which lead to the same experiences and emotions. It's so important to be conscious of what you are thinking, otherwise automatic programming is running your life, rather than conscious choices. Making different choices means that you may feel uncomfortable for a while, because it's not your familiar behavior, but this is how you change the old unhelpful pattern of behavior and install neurological patterns of new behavior.

Start visualizing your new future self, rehearse the new way of being, imagine yourself being and doing all that you want to be and achieve. See your behavior and actions matching your intention.

Remember the Law of Attraction is always working. You can only attract what you are in harmony with, what is vibrating in alignment with the signals you are sending out. The analogy that resonates with me is that you can't pick up a country & western radio station while tuned into a rap music station. At any time, all kinds of music is being broadcast into your home. The only reason you can't hear it is that your radio is not switched on and tuned in. It's the same with you. Direct your focus, thoughts and internal language into what you want and not what you don't. If negative thoughts come into your mind, notice them with interest then let them float away while you focus again on your intended outcome. Think of it like moving house. You are leaving behind your old apartment (old way of thinking) and moving into a beautiful luxury home with a pool and sweeping drive (your new way of thinking). For a few times you may drive back to the old apartment out of habit, and all you need to think is, "Oh, I don't live here anymore", and you turn your car around and go to the beautiful new home.

You can have a happy fulfilling life. You have so many talents and the world will benefit by your presence. See this as true for you. Don't ever give up. See challenges or setbacks as an opportunity to learn and grow. Keep studying successful people and reading inspirational books and enjoy your journey of change.

At the end of each day think about what you did well and praise yourself for that, think what you've learned to do differently next time, and think of at least 3 things to be grateful for.

Finally, know that *You are Awesome*!

Realize that failure isn't bad. You may not succeed the first time, but do not allow that to stop you. Don't ever give up because giving up will never get you closer to your goal. Persistence is key.

REFERENCES

Lidiya, K., Rooks, S., Dowdell, S., Mafu, S., & Carter, L. (2015, March 5). 9 things that stop you from achieving your goals. Retrieved from Addicted2success.com website: https://addicted2success.com/success-advice/9-things-that-stop-you-from-achieving-your-goals/

Self esteem. (n.d.). Retrieved from Gov.au website: https://www.betterhealth.vic.gov.au/health/healthyliving/self-esteem

Signs of low self-esteem. (n.d.). Retrieved from Webmd.com website: https://www.webmd.com/mental-health/signs-low-self-esteem

25 quick ways to reduce stress. (2014, December 16). Retrieved from Colorado.edu website: https://www.colorado.edu/law/25-quick-ways-reduce-stress

Holland, K. (2018, September 19). Anxiety: Causes, symptoms, treatment, and more. Retrieved from Healthline.com website: https://www.healthline.com/health/anxiety

Overview - Generalised anxiety disorder in adults. (n.d.). Retrieved from Nhs.uk website: https://www.nhs.uk/mental-health/conditions/generalised-anxiety-disorder/overview/

Realbuzz Team. (2017, October 27). Top 10 Most Bizarre Phobias.

Retrieved from Realbuzz.com website: https://www.realbuzz.com/articles-interests/health/article/top-10-most-bizarre-phobias/

Star, K. (n.d.). The benefits of anxiety and nervousness. Retrieved from Verywellmind.com website: https://www.verywellmind.com/benefits-of-anxiety-2584134

Debbie Hampton, C. (2016, March 23). How your thoughts change your brain, cells, and genes. Retrieved from Huffpost.com website: https://www.huffpost.com/entry/how-your-thoughts-change-your-brain-cells-and-genes_b_9516176

Lejuwaan, J. (2009, July 20). How your thoughts program your cells. Retrieved from *Highexistence.com* website: https://highexistence.com/thoughts-program-cells/

Rosenberg, J. (2019, March 12). 5 irrational thinking patterns that could be dragging you down — and how to start challenging them. Retrieved from *Ted.com* website: https://ideas.ted.com/5-irrational-thinking-patterns-that-could-be-dragging-you-down-and-how-to-start-challenging-them/

Ruth. (2012, June 21). Five tips for changing the way you look at things. Retrieved from Ruthbowers.com website: https://ruthbowers.com/five-tips-for-changing-the-way-you-look-at-thngs/

6 things that happen when you bottle up your emotions. (2020, September 6). Retrieved from Healthshots.com website: https://www.healthshots.com/mind/emotional-health/6-things-that-happen-when-you-bottle-up-your-emotions/

Abraham hicks - what do we mean by vibration. (2008, September 8). Retrieved from https://www.youtube.com/watch?v=LHjKEZJxMao

Abraham hicks teachings: How to manifest your desires. (2016, November 7). Retrieved from Thepathtoawesomeness.com website: https://thepathtoawesomeness.com/ask-and-it-is-given/

Antoinettecamilleri, V. A. P. (2019, August 11). 15 ways to raise your vibration. Retrieved from Antoinettecamilleri.com website: https://antoinettecamilleri.com/2019/08/11/raise-your-vibration/

Barrett, B. (2020, November 23). 5 ways to improve your self-worth and raise your vibration — awakened adulting. Retrieved from

Awakenedadulting.com website: https://www.awakenedadulting.-com/blog/5-ways-to-improve-your-self-worth-and-raise-your-vibration

How to be more confident and raise your vibration the holistic way. (2018, June 28). Retrieved from Breakfastcriminals.com website: https://www.breakfastcriminals.com/how-to-be-more-confident-9-ways-to-raise-your-vibration-first-thing-in-the-morning/

The relationship between energy and self-confidence. (n.d.). Retrieved from Universalclass.com website: https://www.universal-class.com/articles/self-help/the-relationship-between-energy-and-self-confidence.htm

Ratliff, J. (2016, November 15). To anyone who struggles with "letting go" - personal growth - medium. Retrieved from Personal Growth website: https://medium.com/personal-growth/to-anyone-who-struggles-with-letting-go-ed5bf12fb1e6

DeMers, J. (2015, July 1). How to change your mindset to see problems as opportunities. Retrieved from Inc website: https://www.inc.-com/jayson-demers/how-to-change-your-mindset-to-see-problems-as-opportunities.html

Cherry, K. (n.d.). Problem-solving strategies and obstacles. Retrieved from Verywellmind.com website: https://www.verywell-mind.com/problem-solving-2795008

How to solve daily life problems - anxiety Canada. (2019, April 17). Retrieved from Anxietycanada.com website: https://www.anxi-etycanada.com/articles/how-to-solve-daily-life-problems/

Women influencing business: Using your problem solving skills. (2011, November 18). Retrieved from Kellerinstitute.com website: https://www.kellerinstitute.com/content/women-influencing-busi-ness-using-your-problem-solving-skills

Discover why happiness comes from solving problems (and three simple steps to make it happen). (n.d.). Retrieved from Healthymov-ing.com website: https://healthymoving.com/blog/yoga/discover-why-happiness-comes-from-solving-problems-and-three-simple-steps-to-make-it-happen/

Benefits of Goal Setting. (2015, July 12). Retrieved from Thep-

ter.com/development-series/skill-builder/personal-
effectiveness/goal-setting/benefits-of-goal-setting/

Knobelman, D., & Harpham, B. (2013, August 29). How to set goals
and achieve them successfully. Retrieved from Lifehack.org website:
https://www.lifehack.org/articles/productivity/how-set-goals-10-
steps-stay-focused.html

The importance, benefits, and value of goal setting. (2019, June
14). Retrieved from Positivepsychology.com website: https://posi-
tivepsychology.com/benefits-goal-setting/

Mind visualization technique for building confidence & overcoming fear. (n.d.). Retrieved from Mindtosucceed.com website:
https://www.mindtosucceed.com/mind-visualization.html

Self confidence tip: Vision board & reflection. (n.d.). Retrieved
from Pricelessprofessional.com website: https://www.pricelesspro-
fessional.com/self-confidence-tip-vision-board-reflection.html

Visualization. (n.d.). Retrieved from Mindtools.com website:
https://www.mindtools.com/pages/article/newHTE_81.htm

Williams, S. (n.d.). Mental Rehearsal. Retrieved from Wright.edu
website:
http://www.wright.edu/~scott.williams/LeaderLetter/rehearsal.htm

Boam, P. J. (2018). *The art of journaling: Discover how journaling can
heal your life*. North Charleston, SC: Createspace Independent
Publishing Platform.

Bojan. (2018, April 16). The forgotten art of journaling and three
reasons to start. Retrieved from Alphaefficiency.com website:
https://alphaefficiency.com/art-of-journaling

Glasgow, Y. (2019, April 29). The Art and Importance of Journaling. Retrieved from Lifesavvy.com website: https://www.lifesavvy.-
com/1768/the-art-and-importance-of-journaling/

A Seven-Step Prescription for Self-Love. (n.d.). *Psychology Today*.
Retrieved from https://www.psychologytoday.com/us/blog/get-
hardy/201203/seven-step-prescription-self-love

Chopra, N. (2020, February 13). 10 tangible & thought-provoking
ways to practice self-love. Retrieved from Mindbodygreen.com

134

website: https://www.mindbodygreen.com/0-12428/10-wonderful-ways-to-practice-selflove.html

Edwards, T. (2020, January 31). 5 ways to accept your body and love yourself. Retrieved from Besthealthmag.ca website: https://www.besthealthmag.ca/article/body-positivity/

Stenvinkel, M. (2018, February 22). Be good to yourself: 10 powerful ways to practice self-love. Retrieved from Tinybuddha.com website: https://tinybuddha.com/blog/be-good-to-yourself-10-powerful-ways-to-practice-self-love/

Our body language communicates - Pegasus NLP. (2017, February 16). Retrieved from Nlp-now.co.uk website: https://nlp-now.co.uk/always-communicating/

(N.d.). Retrieved from Nytimes.com website: https://www.nytimes.com/2014/05/25/magazine/a-revolutionary-approach-to-treating-ptsd.html

5 good reasons to stop pleasing others and make yourself A priority. (2019, July 29). Retrieved from Iheartintelligence.com website: https://iheartintelligence.com/reasons-to-stop-pleasing-others/

49 ways to say no to anyone (when you don't want to be A jerk). (2016, July 28). Retrieved from Com.au website: https://www.career-faqs.com.au/news/news-and-views/how-to-say-no-to-anyone

Grothaus, M. (2015, December 4). Your ultimate guide to saying "no" to people you can't say "no" to. Retrieved from Fastcompany.com website: https://www.fastcompany.com/3053996/your-ultimate-guide-to-saying-no-to-people-you-cant-say-no-to

Tong, L. (2016, July 6). 10 surprising reasons to stop trying to please everyone. Retrieved from Tinybuddha.com website: https://tinybuddha.com/blog/10-surprising-reasons-stop-trying-please-everyone/

Jiang, S., & Ngien, A. (2020). The effects of Instagram use, social comparison, and self-esteem on social anxiety: A survey study in Singapore. *Social Media + Society*, 6(2), 205630512091248.

Cohen, J. (2018, November 30). Four ways your inner circle is crucial to your success. *Forbes Magazine*. Retrieved from https://www.forbes.com/sites/jennifercohen/2018/11/30/four-ways-your-inner-circle-is-crucial-to-your-success/

How your circle of friends influence who you become. (2013, October 29). Retrieved from Simonalexanderong.com website: https://www.simonalexanderong.com/2013/10/how-your-circle-of-friends-influence-who-you-become/

Why your inner circle should stay small, and how to shrink it. (2020, November 26). Retrieved from Cleverism.com website: https://www.cleverism.com/why-your-inner-circle-should-stay-small-and-how-to-shrink-it/

Morin, A. (2019, April 1). 7 reasons you allow people to mistreat you. Retrieved from Inc website: https://www.inc.com/amy-morin/7-reasons-you-spend-time-with-people-who-treat-you-poorly.html

Winter, E. (2015, June 29). Why do people behave the way they do? Retrieved from Behavioraleconomics.com website: https://www.behavioraleconomics.com/why-do-people-behave-the-way-they-do/

Penners. (n.d.). Choosing the best clothing for your skin tone. Retrieved from Pennersinc.com website: https://www.pennersinc.com/blogs/penners-blog/choosing-the-best-clothing-for-your-skin-tone

Prince, A., & Henry, B. (2014, September 30). 6 essential ways to start dressing with confidence. Retrieved from Lifehack.org website: https://www.lifehack.org/articles/productivity/6-essential-ways-start-dressing-with-confidence.html

5 top ways to act confident (even when you're not) - bidsketch. (2016, May 13). Retrieved from Bidsketch.com website: https://www.bidsketch.com/blog/everything-else/act-confident/

Barnes, Z. (2016, January 5). 9 ways to fake confidence until you actually believe it. Retrieved from SELF website: https://www.self.com/story/10-ways-to-fake-confidence-until-you-actually-believe-it

Burkeman, O. (2012, December 6). According to "self perception theory," imitating confident people makes you more confident. *Business Insider*. Retrieved from https://www.businessinsider.com/acting-confident-makes-you-more-conficent-2012-12

(c) Copyright skillsyouneed.com 2011-. (n.d.). Building Confidence. Retrieved from Skillsyouneed.com website: https://www.skillsyouneed.com/ps/confidence.html

Clear, J. (2013, July 25). Body language hacks: Be confident and reduce stress in 2 minutes. Retrieved from Jamesclear.com website: https://jamesclear.com/body-language-how-to-be-confident

Fake it 'til you make it: Why faking confidence is actually A really good strategy at work. (n.d.). Retrieved from Psychologicalscience.org website: https://www.psychologicalscience.org/news/fake-it-til-you-make-it-why-faking-confidence-is-actually-a-really-good-strategy-at-work.html

How to boost your confidence. (n.d.). Retrieved from Thefutur.com website: https://thefutur.com/blog/boost-self-confidence-emulate-someone

Humphrey, J. (2019, March 15). 6 ways to fake confidence when you feel insecure. Retrieved from Fastcompany.com website: https://www.fastcompany.com/90318159/6-ways-to-fake-confidence-when-you-feel-insecure

May, K. T. (n.d.). Some examples of how power posing can actually boost your confidence. Retrieved from Ted.com website: https://blog.ted.com/10-examples-of-how-power-posing-can-work-to-boost-your-confidence/

MJ, Kensi Science of People, & Aggarwal, M. (2019, March 26). How to be more confident: 11 scientific strategies for more confidence. Retrieved from Scienceofpeople.com website: https://www.scienceofpeople.com/how-to-be-confident/

Rykert, L. (2019, March 12). 2 confidence-boosting power poses for your next job interview. Retrieved from Localwise.com website: https://www.localwise.com/a/208-2-confidence-boosting-power-poses-for-your-next-job-interview

Shana Lebowitz, M. R. (2015, December 22). The "power poses" that will instantly boost your confidence levels. Retrieved from Inc website: https://www.inc.com/business-insider/amy-cuddy-the-poses-that-will-boost-your-confidence.html

(N.d.). Retrieved from Carriecheadle.com website: https://carriec-headle.com/want-to-be-more-confident-start-acting-like-it/

Benefits of failure. (2020, June 23). Retrieved from Kingfisher-intl.com website: https://www.kingfisherintl.com/2020/06/23/bene-fits-of-failure/

Koulogeorge, P. (2017, November 20). The surprising benefits of failure. *Forbes Magazine*. Retrieved from https://www.forbes.-com/sites/forbescommunicationscouncil/2017/11/20/the-surpris-ing-benefits-of-failure/

Seff. (2018, July 7). 7 very surprising benefits of failure. Retrieved from Seffsaid.com website: https://seffsaid.com/benefits-of-failure/

Yin Yang - Everything About Yin and Yang & Balancing Life. (2007, August 11). Retrieved from Personaltao.com website: https://personaltao.com/taoism/what-is-yin-yang/

Job burnout: How to spot it and take action. (2020, November 20). Retrieved from Mayoclinic.org website: https://www.mayoclin-ic.org/healthy-lifestyle/adult-health/in-depth/burnout/art-20046642

Melinda. (n.d.). *Burnout prevention and treatment - HelpGuide.Org.* Retrieved from https://www.helpguide.org/articles/stress/burnout-prevention-and-recovery.htm

Food & your mood: How food affects mental health - Aetna. (n.d.). Retrieved from Aetna.com website: https://www.aetna.com/health-guide/food-affects-mental-health.html

Robertson, R. (2017, June 27). Why the gut microbiome is crucial for your health. Retrieved from Healthline.com website: https://www.healthline.com/nutrition/gut-microbiome-and-health

Schultz, R. (2018, April 18). Here's what these women ate to treat their anxiety and depression. Retrieved from Healthline.com website: https://www.healthline.com/health/best-diets-for-mental-health

The gut-brain connection. (2012, March 27). Retrieved from Harvard.edu website: https://www.health.harvard.edu/diseases-and-conditions/the-gut-brain-connection

The Microbiome. (2017, August 16). Retrieved from Harvard.edu website: https://www.hsph.harvard.edu/nutritionsource/microbiome/

(N.d.). Retrieved from Washington.edu website: https://depts.washington.edu/ceeh/downloads/FF_Microbiome.pdf

11 scientific benefits of being outdoors. (2015, November 2). Retrieved from Mentalfloss.com website: https://www.mentalfloss.com/article/70548/11-scientific-benefits-being-outdoors

Advanced Neurotherapy, P. C. (n.d.). 4 reasons why walking outside benefits the brain. Retrieved from Advancedneurotherapy.com website: https://www.advancedneurotherapy.com/blog/2015/09/10/walking-outside-brain

Cronkleton, E. (2019, November 7). Working out every day: Guidelines, safety, and more. Retrieved from Healthline.com website: https://www.healthline.com/health/exercise-fitness/working-out-every-day

Eleesha Lockett, M. S. (2019, August 30). What is grounding and can it help improve your health? Retrieved from Healthline.com website: https://www.healthline.com/health/grounding

Exercise, lifestyle and the lymphatic system. (n.d.). Retrieved from Cpandr.co.uk website: https://www.cpandr.co.uk/2018/03/20/exercise-lifestyle-and-the-lymphatic-system/

More evidence that exercise can boost mood. (2019, May 1). Retrieved from Harvard.edu website: https://www.health.harvard.edu/mind-and-mood/more-evidence-that-exercise-can-boost-mood

Five ways mindfulness meditation is good for your health. (n.d.). Retrieved from Berkeley.edu website: https://greatergood.berkeley.edu/article/item/five_ways_mindfulness_meditation_is_good_for_your_health

Cooper, B. B. (2013, August 21). What is meditation & how does it affects our brains? Retrieved from Buffer.com website: https://buffer.com/resources/how-meditation-affects-your-brain/

Patel, D. (2017, March 2). Zenful Spirit22 successful people who meditate. Retrieved from Zenfulspirit.com website: https://zenfulspirit.com/2017/03/02/22-successful-people-meditate/

10 super practical ways to practice gratitude that will change your life - Happier. (n.d.). Retrieved from Happier.com website:

https://www.happier.com/blog/gratitude-skill-here-are-10-super-practical-ways-practice-it-will-change-your-life/

Giving thanks can make you happier. (2011, November 22). Retrieved from Harvard.edu website: https://www.health.harvard.edu/healthbeat/giving-thanks-can-make-you-happier

Top 11 Ways that gratitude enhances your life. (2018, August 1). Retrieved from Liveyourtruestory.com website: https://www.liveyourtruestory.com/top-11-ways-that-gratitude-enhances-your-life-confidence/

What we know about gratitude and giving back. (n.d.). *Psychology Today*. Retrieved from https://www.psychologytoday.com/us/blog/evidence-based-living/201706/what-we-know-about-gratitude-and-giving-back

Why you should be thankful for your failures. (2019, November 25). Retrieved from Teamzy.com website: https://teamzy.com/why-you-should-still-be-thankful-for-your-failures/

Beard, C. (2018, October 7). 25 daily affirmations to improve your mindset - the blissful mind. Retrieved from Theblissfulmind.com website: https://theblissfulmind.com/positive-affirmations-list/

Canfield, J. (2016, September 21). Daily affirmations for success - examples & tips. Retrieved from Jackcanfield.com website: https://www.jackcanfield.com/blog/practice-daily-affirmations/

Canfield, J. (2021, February 25). Using the law of attraction for joy, relationships, money & more [guide]. Retrieved from Jackcanfield.com website: https://www.jackcanfield.com/blog/using-the-law-of-attraction/

Positive daily affirmations: Is there science behind it? (2019, March 4). Retrieved from Positivepsychology.com website: https://positivepsychology.com/daily-affirmations/

5 health benefits of daily meditation according to science. (2019, June 19). Retrieved from Positivepsychology.com website: https://positivepsychology.com/benefits-of-meditation/

Bailey, K. (2018, July 31). 5 powerful health benefits of journaling. Retrieved from Intermountainhealthcare.org website: https://intermountainhealthcare.org/blogs/topics/live-well/2018/07/5-powerful-health-benefits-of-journaling/

(c) Copyright skillsyouneed.com 2011-. (n.d.). Self-Motivation. Retrieved from Skillsyouneed.com website: https://www.skillsyouneed.com/ps/self-motivation.html

Grate, R. (2015, February 17). Science shows something surprising about people who still journal. Retrieved from Mic.com website: https://www.mic.com/p/science-shows-something-surprising-about-people-who-still-journal-16207322

Link, R., MS, & RD. (2017, August 30). 13 benefits of yoga that are supported by science. Retrieved from Healthline.com website: https://www.healthline.com/nutrition/13-benefits-of-yoga

Rebecca Joy Stanborough, M. F. A. (2020, April 1). Benefits of music on body, mind, relationships & more. Retrieved from Healthline.com website: https://www.healthline.com/health/benefits-of-music

Why reading can be good for mental health. (2018, September 4). Retrieved from Mhfaengland.org website: https://mhfaengland.org/mhfa-centre/blog/reading-good-mental-health/

ABOUT THE AUTHOR

Kate is a trained Coach and NLP Practitioner specializing in helping people overcome self-doubt and step into their full potential. She lives with her two sons in California.

Intrigued by the power of the mind, and with a passion to help people realize their worth, Kate shows you how to stop settling and reconnect to your confident self to live the life you truly desire.

Having overcome her own limiting beliefs and thought patterns, as well as becoming a young widow, Kate's purpose is to help others awaken their inner strength and live life on their terms.

Made in the USA
Las Vegas, NV
13 January 2024

84316360R00085